Books should be returned on or before the
last date stamped below.

THE
HOUNDSDITCH MURDERS

&

The Siege of Sidney Street

By the same author

I SPY BLUE

THE
HOUNDSDITCH
MURDERS

&

The Siege of Sidney Street

DONALD RUMBELOW

ST MARTIN'S PRESS
MACMILLAN

SBN: 333 14870 3

Library of Congress catalog card no.: 73–83129

First published 1973 by
MACMILLAN LONDON LTD
London and Basingstoke
Associated companies in New York Dublin
Melbourne Johannesburg & Madras

Printed in Great Britain by
WESTERN PRINTING SERVICES LTD
Bristol

*To my Mother
and
to the memory of
my Father*

Contents

List of Illustrations

List of Maps

Preface

SEVERAL years ago, chance put in my way the police documents on which this book is largely based. They were scattered about in old cardboard boxes, thickly coated with dust, and had survived not only the Blitz but years of neglect; they were earmarked for destruction. Several months of spare time was spent trying to put them in some sort of order. The maps had crumbled and had to be restored. (The binder thought they had been baked!) Later I thought I would write a short account of the 'siege' from these documents. I didn't expect to find anything new as the story was so well known. However, once I had started to work on the papers, the errors and omissions in former versions of the story became only too apparent; it is for this reason that I have kept almost exclusively to the original documents and quoted, with few exceptions, only from incidents in which the writers were personally involved and when they were not speaking from hearsay.

Some of the more personal documents have survived only in the very stilted translations which were made at the time. I have preferred to paraphrase these letters, which have been used very sparingly and which do not affect the main line of the story, rather than quote from them direct.

I should like to thank the following for their help and encouragement in the writing of this book; L. C. Dixon Esq. for memories of his grandfather Sergeant Dixon, who was awarded the King's Police Medal for his bravery in the Tottenham Outrage; W. J. and L. J. Piper for memories of their father, Police Constable Walter Piper, who went to investigate the 'noises' in Exchange Buildings; G. A. Freeman for information about his brother-in-law, Jacob Peters, and his niece, May; the delightful Mrs Leader, whom I can never think of except as

Bessie Jacobs, as she was when she lived in Exchange Buildings and saw the murdered policemen and later gave evidence at the trial; Sam Hart, who saw the men escaping and lifted the dying Police Sergeant out of the doorway; Keith Andreang for taping documents; Donald MacCormick for help with Peter's background; Dale Wilkinson for photographs; Miss Betty Masters, Assistant Keeper of Records at the Guildhall Records Office, for helping to trace the payment to the Sidney Street informer; the Commissioner of the City of London Police and the Commissioner of the Metropolitan Police.

The last two debts are the heaviest ones. To my wife Polly, who has not only had to listen to the story for several years but had to type it; and to James Wright, who nearly broke down under the plethora of false names. Without them the book would not have been written. Both can rest easy until the next time.

D.R.

List of Characters

I HAVE noted the main characters in the story in the hope that this will be helpful to the reader. Many of the anarchists operated under various aliases. I have, for interest, given them in parenthesis.

WANTED MEN, RELATIONS AND FRIENDS

Tottenham Outrage
Fogel, Jacob (real name Jan Sprohe, alias Grishka Sander; surname also spelt Vogel)
Hefeld, Paul (nickname 'Elephant')
Jacob (surname Lepidus or Lapidus?)
Vanoveitch, Evan (?Jan Janoff Palameiko, nickname 'Bifsteks')

Houndsditch Murders
Dubof, Yourka (real name Yourka Laiwin)
Federoff, Osip
Gardstein, George (also P. Morin, Poolka Mourrewitz or Mourremitz, or Mouremtzoff, George Garstin; carried passports in names of Schafshi Khan and Yanis Karlowitch Stentzel)
Gershon, Betsy (lodger, 100 Sidney Street, where Svaars and Joseph hid; she was Joseph's mistress)
Hoffman, Karl (also Janis Trautman, Chochol and Masais; carried passport in name of Peter Trohimtchick, which was an alias used by Fritz Svaars)
'Joseph', *see* Sokoloff, William
Levi, Joe, *see* Smoller, Max
Milstein, Luba (Svaars' mistress)

Molchanoff (or Molacoff), Pavell (friend of Peter Piaktow)

Peters, Jacob (cousin of Fritz Svaars)

Piaktow, Peter (alias Peter Schtern; 'Peter the Painter')

Rosen, John (also John Zelin or Tzelin, nickname 'the Barber')

Smoller, Max (also Marx or Marks Smellor; rented 11 Exchange Buildings as Joe Levi)

Sokaloff, William (surname also spelt Sokaloff, Sokolow, Sokolov and Solokoff; commonly known as 'Joseph')

Svaars, Fritz (cousin to Jacob Peters; also known as Karl Davidoff Dumnek, Louis Lambert and Peter (?) Trohimtchick, which was an alias also used by Hoffman)

Trassjonsky, Sara ('Rosa'; carried passport in name of Sara [Davidowna Tuwiena] daughter of David Tuwic Treschau)

Vassilleva, Nina (also Lena Vasilev; carried passport in name of Minna, daughter of Indrik Gristis)

Police and Witnesses

Abrahams, Mr and Mrs (tenants of 12 Exchange Buildings)

—, Solomon (their son)

Bentley, Police Sergeant Robert (murdered at Houndsditch)

Bluestein, Mrs (landlady, 102 Sidney Street)

Brown, Wolf and Fanny (36 Lindley Street, where Hoffman lived)

Bryant, Police Sergeant (wounded at Houndsditch)

Choat, Police Constable Walter (murdered at Houndsditch)

Clemens (or Clements), Mr and Mrs (lodgers of Fleishmann's)

Dixon, Detective (involved at Tottenham)

Eagles, Police Constable (involved at Tottenham)

Fleishmann (or Flieschmann), Rebecca (landlady, 100 Sidney Street)

—, Samuel (her husband)

Freedman, Dr Mengle (acquaintance of Nina Vassilleva)

Gordon, Isaac (Nina Vassilleva's landlord)

—, Fanny (his wife)

—, Polly (their daughter)

Harris, H. S. (jeweller)

—, Harry (his son)

Hart, Sam (witness at Houndsditch)

Hayes, Chief Inspector (stationed at Bishopsgate on the night of the Houndsditch murders)

Jacobs, Harry (tenant, Exchange Buildings)

—, Bessie (his sister)

Johnstone, Dr Nelson (Sidney Street)

Joscelyne, Ralph (boy murdered at Tottenham)

Katz, Max (landlord, 59 Grove Street)

—, Mrs (his wife)

Kempler, Jacob (44 Gold Street, where Gardstein lodged as P. Morin)

Keyworth, Albert (Schnurmann's factory wages-clerk)

Leeson, Detective Sergeant Benjamin (wounded at Sidney Street)

Levy, Isaac (witness at Houndsditch)

Martin, Police Constable James (Houndsditch)

Mulvaney, Divisional Superintendent (Metropolitan Police)

Newman, Police Constable (Tottenham)

Ottaway, Detective Superintendent John (City)

Parker, Ada (tenant, Exchange Buildings)

Petter, Elsa (Dubof's landlady)

Pilenas, Casimir (interpreter from Thames Police Court)

—, Peter (his brother)

Piper, Police Constable Walter (Houndsditch)

Reitman, Morris (lodger, 36 Lindley Street)

—, Mrs 'Grobber'

Scanlon, Dr John (attended Gardstein)

Schiemann (also Sheinmann, Shiesmann, Schiesbann), David and Mrs (lodgers of Fleishmann's)

Silisteanu, Michail (rented 10 Exchange Buildings)

Smolensky, Abraham (Svaars' landlord at Newcastle Place)

Stark, Superintendent John (City)

Strongman, Police Constable Arthur (identified Peters at Houndsditch)

Thompson, Detective Inspector

Tucker, Police Sergeant (murdered at Houndsditch)

Tyler, Police Constable (murdered at Tottenham)

Weil, Max (trader in Houndsditch)
Wensley, Detective Inspector Frederick Porter ('Weasel')
Wilson, Joseph (chauffeur, Schnurmann's rubber factory)
Woodhams, Police Constable Ernest (wounded at Houndsditch)

Informers
Perelman, Charles (also spelt Pearlman; landlord at Great
    Garden Street and Wellesley Street)
Tomacoff, Nicholas (also spelt Tomazeff; balalaika-player)

I

The Tottenham Outrage

In 1909 nearly two million Londoners were officially classed as poor or very poor. Most of them lived in the East End. For centuries the City of London's stringent corporate and guild restrictions had forced new labour to live and work on the open marshland outside the City wall. Immigrants fleeing continental persecutions, notably the seventeenth-century Huguenots, settled in East London. Steadily the number of immigrants increased. By the end of the nineteenth century the brickfields and the pleasant weavers'-houses had become rack-rented ghettos. Nearly fifty per cent of the workers paid from a quarter to half of their wages for poky little one-room hovels for themselves and their families.

From the 1870s the East End began to expand to the east and to the north. The railways brought growth to the villages on the periphery of London. The old village main streets with their half-timbered cottages and bow-fronted homes on either side were rapidly expanded from behind with two-storeyed houses, mostly jerry-built. Soon these became microcosms of the East End. Walthamstow was called Little Bethnal Green. The familiar pattern of brawling, street markets with naphtha flares, nightly drunkenness was once more repeated. Rapidly these new areas degenerated into slums. Fresh waves of immigrants from central and eastern Europe, from Poland and Tsarist Russia, moved into these areas in the 1890s and the first decade of the twentieth century. Wages, which were already low, were depressed still more. Unable to compete at these low rates, the workers in some areas rioted. In Tottenham, in 1902, they smashed factory windows with stones. They achieved nothing. Seven years later large numbers of immigrants were still being employed by the rubber factory, Schnurmann's, in Chestnut Road at the corner of Tottenham High Road. The factory façade of bleak quarried stone, now painted grey, was more suited to a prison than to a factory, despite the ornamental pine-apples on the roof. The only openings in the street wall were some small mitre-windows. Between the side walls of the gate was stretched a thick cable and from it was suspended, like a pendant, a monster gas-lamp faceted with panes of glass like a diamond. The gates beneath it had a forbidding fringe of metal spikes.

On Saturday, 23 January 1909 these gates were open. Two young political refugees from the Baltic state of Latvia, Paul Hefeld and Jacob, both in their twenties, one dark and the other fair, were lounging on the pavement outside, one on either side of the entrance, insolently eyeing the police station opposite as they waited, with guns in their pockets, for the factory car to return from the London & South Western Bank in Hackney with the week's wages, about £80, as it did every Saturday morning at 10.30.

The car was a few minutes late. As it turned the corner they noted the gleaming brasswork, the monster headlamps and the carriage lamps on the hood supports. The rear of the car was boxed in with leather like a hansom cab, which it closely resembled, and the only protection the driver had from the weather was from the roof and the full-length glass panel in front. In wet weather he had to look through an oval incision in the glass. Huddled behind the glass (the front half of the car had no doors) were the driver, Joseph Wilson, in his heavy motor-coat and gauntlets, and the seventeen-year-old wages-clerk Albert Keyworth.

Keyworth paused as he stepped onto the pavement with the wages bag in his hand. Seeing the two men on either side of the entrance made him suspicious. Hefeld saw him hesitate and nodded his head in greeting. Keyworth nodded back as he recognised Hefeld as somebody who had recently worked at the factory. He knew him by sight but did not know his name. Nobody did. Hefeld had contemptuously refused to give it. The management had been indifferent so long as he did the work. All immigrants lied anyway. In the blank name-space on his time-sheets they put down, in allusion to his great bulk, his nickname 'Elephant'.

As the car pulled away Keyworth walked across the pavement to the factory yard. Before he could reach the entrance Jacob's arm locked around his throat from behind. Keyworth shouted and plunged forward with Jacob clinging to his back. Frantically he tried to throw him off but Jacob hung on and with his free hand tore at Keyworth's arm and at the canvas bag he held just out of reach. Wilson heard the shout, and as the two men staggered backwards into the roadway he leaped out of the car and ran towards them. He threw his arms round Jacob's head and pulled him off the boy. Then, throwing all his weight forward, he tried to force the man's head down between his knees. In so doing, he himself was completely off balance and a sudden sideways movement rolled him over Jacob's head and shoulders onto his back. As he sprawled, momentarily winded, in the roadway he looked up and saw Hefeld, who until then had taken no part in the fighting, moving towards him with a gun in his hand. Jacob, meanwhile, had managed to wrench away the wages bag from the boy and was also pulling out a gun.

Hefeld fired several times in rapid succession. Wilson rolled desperately over and over shouting for help. Miraculously he was not hit. His ankle-length motor-coat was riddled with holes, and a slanting shot across his stomach cut through everything he was wearing including his vest.

The police station is on the corner of Tottenham High Road and Chestnut Road. From the office window there is a clear view across the road to Schnurmann's. The shots were heard inside the station and two policemen on Reserve, 403'N' Tyler and 510'N' Newman, ran into the High Road. 'Guv'nor, you're wanted,' shouted a passer-by and pointed down Chestnut Road. They ran round the corner just in time to see a passer-by, a burly stoker called George Smith, bring Jacob crashing to the ground with a flying tackle. Smith had run down the street using the car as a cover and had taken the two gunmen completely by surprise. As Hefeld spun round to face this new threat the driver seized his opportunity, staggered to his feet, and ran towards the policemen less than forty yards away.

Smith and Jacob were still wrestling on the ground, with Smith on top, and there was not even time for Hefeld to take aim. He straddled the two men and fired four times at Smith's head. Two shots went through his cap tearing his scalp, one completely missed and the other slightly wounded him in the fleshy part of the collar bone. Incredibly Jacob was not hit. Catching hold of the startled Smith by the throat he rolled him over and grabbed the wages bag. Hefeld fired once more and then the two of them began running down Chestnut Road with the two policemen close on their heels.

Some passers-by joined in the chase. One woman further down the road, buying greengroceries at her gate, flung a potato at them as they ran past. More help came from the police station, which was also a section house. Some of the night-duty men were woken by the shots. Others heard Police Constable Bond, who had been shaving and seen the robbery from an upstairs window, shouting the alarm as he ran downstairs. He grabbed a truncheon, leaped through a window into the yard below, and over a wall into the street. The others quickly followed. Most of them were on foot but some of them commandeered bicycles and pedalled furiously down the road. Most of them had not understood what had happened.

Hefeld and Jacob took the first turning to the left and ran through the small streets of terraced houses towards the marshes by the River Lea. All the time they kept firing back at the policemen on their heels. In Scales Road Tyler and Newman recklessly closed to within nine yards but were again beaten off by the gunmen's fire and forced to shelter behind a stationary dust-cart. Moments later, the factory car turned the corner with

Wilson at the wheel. Newman climbed in while the manager and Tyler ran alongside, holding on to the car as it slowed down to a walking pace. They followed the gunmen into Mitchley Road. As one of them stopped by the Mission Hall to reload Wilson shouted that the gun was empty. Newman excitedly told him to run the gunman down if he could.

Jacob and Hefeld crouched down as the car accelerated towards them. They took careful aim and fired simultaneously. A leather-cutter's wife, who had heard the police whistles and the shots, was standing by her gate with her baby in her arms when the gunmen opened fire. She saw a small boy run to the car for cover as everyone ducked.

One shot tore through Newman's cheek and the lobe of his ear as the bullets smashed the windscreen. Another cut across Wilson's neck and collar and a third burst the car's water-pipe. The small boy had almost reached the car when he lifted his hand to his mouth and fell heavily onto the edge of the pavement. Jacob and Hefeld took to their heels once more. Thrusting the baby into someone's arms, the leather-cutter's wife ran into the roadway and took the child from a passer-by who had picked him up. Blood was trickling from his mouth. Cradling him in her arms she ran to the car, but because of the burst water-pipe it was impossible to drive on. Newman looked bleakly at the child as he dabbed the blood on his cheek and then ran on after Tyler and Bond, who were still dogging Jacob and Hefeld as they headed for the marshes. Somebody with a bicycle took the child to hospital, but it was too late. He was already dead from a slanting shot through the body.

Somebody else was sent back to the police station for firearms. These were locked in a cupboard, but as they had never been wanted nobody knew where the key was kept and the lock had to be smashed. Thrusting the guns into their pockets, more policemen headed for the marshes on bicycles.

The two gunmen were now in Down Road heading towards the marshes. This meant that they had to cross over the railway footbridge by the Council Depot and Refuse Destructor at the end of Down Road; it was surrounded by a wall about five feet high. Concealed by this wall Tyler, Bond and Newman tried to head off their quarry by cutting across some waste ground behind the houses. Tyler, the most athletic of the three, was in the lead when the gunmen ran out from behind the wall. As they converged on the footbridge there was only twenty yards between them.

'Come on; give in, the game's up,' shouted Tyler.

Hefeld turned, lifted his Bergmann automatic and pulled the trigger. Tyler's head snapped back and he fell forward on his face. Newman shouted for a gun as the rest of the pursuers ran up. Snatching one, he ran forward and fired three shots at Jacob and Hefeld as they scrambled over the footbridge.

Tyler was carried to a nearby cottage. The owner's daughter had been kneeling at the back window as the gunmen raced by. 'Look, mama, there's some men racing!' she called. She saw some 'sparks' and the policeman fall to the ground. He was carried into the scullery a few minutes later. Tyler opened his eyes and groaned but could not speak. He rapidly lost consciousness. Nothing could be done for him. The bullet had gone through the right side of his neck and he was bleeding to death.

The Divisional Inspector asked the Superintendent of the Refuse Depot to telephone police headquarters at Stoke Newington for reinforcements while he returned to the station for his horse. Policemen from the surrounding stations were told to converge on Tottenham marshes. Some of them were armed by their station and a few of them borrowed firearms. Most of them were armed only with truncheons.

Jacob and Hefeld continued firing as they crossed the bridge and gained the marshes on the other side. The footpath weaved away in front of them to Stonebridge Lock. The stubby grass underfoot was green in contrast with the bleached acres of wind-beaten rye-grass and couch-grass about them. Scraggy green nettles and brown shafts of sorrel were not so yielding and stood in clumps waist-high, against the wind. As they bobbed along the footpath they could see the black rooftops of the barges moored on the canal. Coming steadily nearer, they gained some height and began to see the brightly painted panels

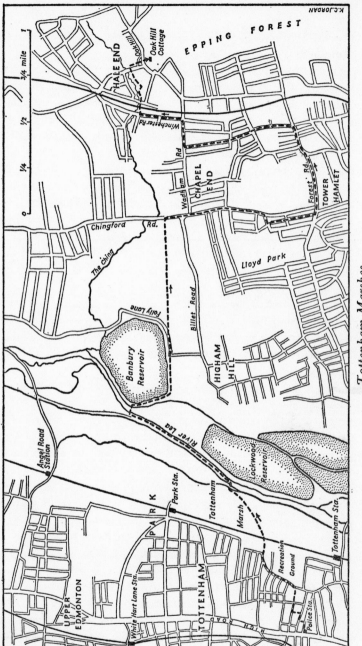

Tottenham Marshes

and the brittle walls of the canal. Behind the canal was the long, even slope of Lockwood Reservoir.

They crossed over Stonebridge Lock. For a few minutes they rested on the gates and fired from the rails at their pursuers. Some footballers on the marsh had now joined in the chase. Crossing over they continued along the footpath on the east side of the canal. The ground sloped down to their right to Tottenham mill-stream about twenty feet below them. Before they could get to the open space around Banbury reservoir they had to cross yet another bridge and this was now threatened by some labourers on the other side of the canal who were demolishing some rifle-butts. Flinging down their picks and shovels they started running along the opposite bank to head them off. Jacob and Hefeld ran parallel with them and, firing continuously across the canal, succeeded in wounding several of them. Once on the bridge they rested and again kept the crowd at bay by firing from the parapet. A policeman crept through the scrub on the mill-stream bank and got within firing range, but his gun was faulty. Before he could get back he was spotted from the bridge and shot in the calf and thigh.

From the bridge, the footpath swept round the south side of Banbury Reservoir. On either side of the footpath was a high fence, and the risk for the pursuers was greatly increased, as once they got between the palings there was no room for them to spread out. Instead they had to keep well back against the fence, especially on the bends, and they could hear shots repeatedly hitting the palings. One man got too close and was shot in the thigh. Through the hedges on the slope of Banbury Reservoir above them, one of the policemen saw a party of sportsmen out duck shooting. He called to them to shoot the man with the green cap (this was Hefeld, who was doing most of the firing) but at first they failed to take in the situation. Some of them then hurried to the top of the reservoir for a better view. Looking down they could see six policemen in front; every time the gunmen fired they took cover. The duck shooters fired through the hedges at Jacob and Hefeld; one of the men was seen to put his hand to his face as though hit and his cap was later found to have been riddled with shot.

Jacob and Hefeld hurried on until they saw the open ground around the base of Higham Hill in front of them. Reaching some cottages they rested once more and then ran across some fields in the direction of Folly Lane. As they cut through the fields and the adjoining allotments they ran into a small gypsy-encampment with two round-top caravans. 'You have some too,' shouted Hefeld and fired at one of the gypsies who ran out. They had now almost reached Billet Road, but as they ran towards it they suddenly saw more of their pursuers appearing in front of them over the hedgerow on bicycles, horses, in motor-cars and on foot.

Forced to retreat once more, the two men hurried on as fast as they could across the fields to Salisbury Hall Farm. They were too exhausted to run. Hefeld was still doing most of the firing. He would halt every so often and use his left arm as a rest for his automatic while Jacob reloaded the other gun. Then they would walk a little way and jog-trot a similar distance. In the farmyard they took temporary shelter behind a haystack. From either side of it they kept firing at their pursuers, who at this point had dropped down to about twenty and had to throw themselves into the furrows as the bullets swept across the field waist-high.

Behind the gunmen was the Chingford Road. Running down it for some two or three miles was a single-track tramline. At various stages there were loops for trams to pass each other. The trams passed Salisbury Hall Farm which was about a mile from Chingford, and on Saturday mornings they were little used. Jacob and Hefeld saw a tram approaching. Suddenly they broke cover and dashed for the road.

As he passed Salisbury Hall Farm the driver of tramcar number 9 saw a crowd of excited people running across the farm in his direction. He could hear cries of 'Murder' and somebody shouting to him to stop. As he slowed down a man (from his story it is not clear who, but the indications are that it was Jacob) jumped over a hedge or ditch and rushed onto

the platform. In his hand he held a revolver and he was calling
to a man who was running along the road about fifty yards
behind the tram. 'Stop,' shouted Jacob, pointing his gun at
the driver and conductor. The driver braked and, as Hefeld ran
nearer, some of the crowd, which now included the duck
shooters, opened fire on the stationary tram with shotguns as
well as revolvers. The tram's three passengers – an elderly man,
a woman and a child – flung themselves face downwards in
the aisle as the windows were shattered and flying glass littered
the interior. The driver, too, was caught in the cross-fire. Convinced that death was inevitable if he stayed where he was, he
managed to scramble up some steps at the front of the tram
without being seen by Jacob and hide behind the seats on the
top deck. The conductor had to stay where he was on the
platform with Jacob until Hefeld scrambled on board. Only
then did Jacob realise that the tram had no driver. Thrusting
his pistol into the conductor's face he told him to drive the tram.
The conductor, unhappily, and quite truthfully, told him that
he had never driven anything in his life. Jacob placed the pistol
against the conductor's head as Hefeld opened fire on the men
behind the hedges, and told him once more to drive the tram.
Knowing that he would almost certainly be shot if he refused
again, the conductor walked to the front of the tram and fum-
bled at the controls as bullets flew about them. As the tram
pulled slowly away Jacob held his gun-barrel against the conductor's cheek and Hefeld kept up a steady fire from the platform at the back. Most of their pursuers were now being left
behind but some were already looking for ways of continuing
the chase.

The conductor's main worry was whether the driver upstairs
would do anything silly to jeopardise his life. He could, if he
wanted to, stop the tram by pressing down the trolly bar and
cutting the circuit. Meanwhile, the conductor racked his brains
to think of some way of bringing the nightmare journey to an
end. Jacob stood by his side the whole time, occasionally turning
and firing at some imaginary pursuer. His ammunition seemed
inexhaustible. No sooner was his magazine empty than he dipped

his hand into his pocket and pulled out a fresh supply. Hefeld came up to the front for a few minutes just as the tram reached a loop and was forced to slow down to let another tram pass in the opposite direction. The woman passenger and the child were able to scramble off unseen, but the elderly man had to stay on. He was becoming increasingly agitated.

The other tram had not gone very far when it was stopped by some of the pursuers running towards it and immediately put into reverse. Meanwhile, the captured tram was fast being caught up by a horse-drawn advertising-cart which had been commandeered by an armed policeman. It came up behind the tram at a sharp trot, but before it could get near enough for the policeman to open fire Hefeld killed the pony with one carefully aimed shot, spilling the occupants into the road and throwing the can of paste which was in the cart on top of them.

As the tram approached a bend in the road the conductor suddenly had an idea. 'You'd better get off here,' he said, 'as there is a police station just round the bend.' Jacob did not know whether to believe him or not and his uncertainty was increased still more by the conductor's apparent indifference. The situation was unexpectedly resolved by the elderly passenger. As the tram came to the bend, Kite's Corner, the strain proved too much for him and he stumbled forward as if he meant to snatch the gun. Jacob was too quick for him. He turned and shot the old man in the throat. As he collapsed in the aisle Jacob and Hefeld leaped off the tram and ran for a milk cart standing by the kerb. The milkman came running towards them and was instantly shot in the chest. They jumped on the milk cart and, lashing the horse with a whip, drove off down Kenilworth Avenue in the direction of Forest Road and Epping Forest.

Somehow they managed to wreck the milk cart. It was said they turned it over taking a corner too fast. Abandoning it they stopped a greengrocer's van and ordered the teenage driver out at gun-point. Jacob grabbed the reins and Hefeld climbed onto the tailboard with both pistols. Hefeld sat with his wrists on his drawn-up knees and the guns hanging limply down. Almost immediately they were chased by some policemen on bicycles, one of them carrying a cutlass, who were part of the larger force steadily closing in. Whenever they came too near Hefeld fired. In Forest Road he shot at a policeman on foot. The policeman immediately chased after them blowing his whistle and within minutes had commandeered a chauffeur-driven car. Two more policemen and two passers-by jumped in from behind. (Later the police had to pay a bill for bending both wings.) The car kept steadily behind the cart. It was never more than a hundred yards away and sometimes crept up to thirty yards whenever one of the passengers wanted to fire the shotgun.

In spite of the savage lashing he was giving the horse – the owner later complained that the pony was so overstrained that he could not work it for four days – Jacob could not work up any more speed. He had not realised that the chain-brake was on and that one of the wheels was running dead. The horse was soon spent, and as the steepness of the road increased it rapidly became clear that they would have to abandon it. They did so in Winchester Road and once more retreated on foot with their pursuers close behind.

A narrow, shallow stream known as the Ching Brook ran under a very tall railway-arch. One bank, on the Winchester Road side of the arch, was open but on the other side were six-foot palings forming part of the boundary of the yard of newly erected houses. The two men ran along the fence not realising that the footpath converged on the fence and got steadily narrower until it disappeared altogether. When they realised their mistake it was too late to turn back and they tried instead to climb over the fence. They were both exhausted by the long chase. Jacob managed to scramble over but Hefeld stumbled and fell back just as the first of the pursuers ran up. Seeing he was about to be captured Hefeld shouted to Jacob to save himself and then fired his gun into his brain. The bullet went in half an inch above the right eye and exploded out through the forehead on the other side. He was still alive. Before he could fire again the gun was wrenched from his fingers. Struggling violently he was overpowered and taken to the Prince of Wales Hospital covered in blood. His shirt was ripped up to bandage his wound. On the way he would not speak beyond remarking that he felt cold.

Jacob, meanwhile, had managed to scramble up the steep incline and cross over the railway line. He cut through Beech Hall Estate, where some houses were being built, ran across Oak Hill, through the hedge, and headed across some fields towards Oak Cottage where he was temporarily lost sight of.

Oak Cottage was a small old-fashioned house belonging to a coal porter, Charles Rolstone, and consisted of four rooms and a lean-to. Mrs Rolstone was home with the children. Shortly after noon, she heard police whistles and went to her front gate and stood there with her little boy. A policeman hurried by looking for Jacob and curtly told her, 'Woman, go in and shut your door; there is a murderer about.' She went back to the cottage and pushed the door of the lean-to which was to the left of the cottage and formed a sort of scullery. To her astonishment she found it locked. She pushed it again and then to her horror saw a blood-stained face and 'wild staring eyes' staring back at her through a hole six inches square at the side of the door. She began to scream. Her two other children, age $2\frac{1}{2}$ and 6, were locked inside with him.

After Jacob had cut across the field he had scrambled over the back fence into Oak Cottage garden and run into the kitchen. He immediately bolted the front door and locked the door of the lean-to. The children were terrified by his blood-stained appearance as he stood in the kitchen drinking from the mug that had been put on the table for them. He savagely told them to be quiet and then went into the sitting-room.

The cottage was hurriedly surrounded. Police Constable Eagles, when he reached Oak Cottage, heard a crowd of people shouting out, 'He has gone into that house.' He borrowed a double-barrelled breech-loading gun from a bystander and went into the scullery. Moments before another policeman had smashed the glass with a brick and gone in and brought out the children. Hearing a noise upstairs, Eagles went into the yard and got a ladder from the garden of the next house. Meanwhile, two detectives, Dixon and Cater, had crept through a

ground-floor window into the cottage. One of the first things
they noticed was the number of sooty handprints on the walls
and furniture. As the chimney was one of the large old-fashioned
type they thought it might be Jacob's hiding-place and fired a
shot up the chimney to flush him out. All they did was to dis-
lodge more soot. Then they moved over to the staircase door
and Dixon slowly crept upstairs to the landing. Cautiously he
opened the front-bedroom door and then sprang back, slam-
ming the door behind him, as he saw Jacob fire. Dixon shouted
to him to surrender and throw out his gun, but Jacob mumbled
that he would do no such thing.

Outside the cottage, Eagles dragged the ladder into the yard
and put it up against the back wall. He climbed up to the bedroom window and opened it. At the suggestion of an onlooker,
a collie dog that was tied up in the yard was passed in to Dixon
and sent up the stairs in the hope that it might flush Jacob out
or at least divert his attention. Eagles, looking in through the
window, saw the dog come onto the landing and then beyond
him Jacob appear in the bedroom doorway pointing a gun at
him. Eagles pulled the trigger of his double-barrelled gun but
nothing happened. He quickly slid down the ladder before
Jacob could fire and tumbled into the house. Jacob had not
fired because he had only two bullets left.

Dixon crept up to the landing again with a double-barrelled
shotgun which someone had passed in through the window.
One of the barrels did not fire, but with the other he peppered
the front-bedroom door with shot. He and Cater then began
firing through the thin door with their revolvers. Creeping
nearer they looked through the bullet holes they had made and
saw Jacob hysterically flinging himself about the room. Eagles
joined them on the landing. According to Dixon, Eagles did
not value his own life as much as he, Dixon, did his, and was
anxious to have a shot. 'Let me have a pop at him,' he begged.

At first Dixon would not hand over his revolver as he wanted
to defend himself. But Eagles begged again and after some
persuasion Dixon allowed him to take it. Eagles, without hesitation, flung his whole weight against the door and burst it

partially open. Thrusting his arm around the door until it was well inside the room, he fired two shots. Jacob was leaping about wildly shouting, 'Come on now.' His face was spattered with blood and his head and shoulders black with soot; he looked like a blood-stained crow. He peered out of the window and instantly every pane of glass was shattered with shot. He flung himself on the bed and tried to pull a sheet over his head. 'Come on now,' he screamed as Eagles shouldered the door open and charged into the room. The two men fired simultaneously. Jacob fell back shot in the head.

The child's bedroom was spattered with blood. The ceiling by the window was ploughed up with shot. The pictures on the opposite wall had been smashed and the floor was littered with fragments of smashed ornaments. Eagles snatched Jacob's pistol out of his hand and Dixon grabbed him by the throat. They dragged him backwards along the floor and downstairs into the yard. The crowd gathered round him as he lay there on his back. Some flicker of life still existed, but for a few minutes only. As he hovered between life and death everyone who saw it remembered the horrible grin on his face. He never stopped grinning. That awful look, with the staring eyes, was still on his face when he died a few minutes later. So intense was the feeling against him that had it not been for the police the crowd, so Dixon believed, would have poured paraffin on him and burned him where he lay.

The chase had lasted more than two hours, and had covered a distance of six miles. Hefeld and Jacob had fired over 400 rounds of ammunition. Two people had been killed and twenty-one others, seven of them policemen, had been wounded or injured in some way. Several of them were in a critical condition.

Up until 4 p.m. Mrs Tyler still expected her husband home to dinner. A friend who had heard that her husband had been shot hurried round to console her, and was startled to find that nobody so far had told her what had happened. He told her that he had heard that there had been a bit of bother and that her husband had been shot in the leg. He had seen a constable being taken to hospital. Mrs Tyler hurriedly put on her coat and set off for the hospital. Before she got there the friend took her into his own home and broke the news that her husband was dead. He was thirty-one. They had been married 12 months.

For some hours nobody knew who the boy was. In the evening somebody heard that a boy named Ralph Joscelyne was missing. A policeman went to the boy's home, taking with him a piece of clothing from the body, and asked the parents if they recognised it. Husband and wife rushed to the hospital. A photograph of the father was taken as he stood outside the coroner's court a few days later. He is standing on the edge of the pavement, rigid with grief. His wife never got over the shock. She kept the shoes her boy was wearing on the day he died. When she herself died, nearly fifty years later, they were buried with her.

On 26 January the inquest opened on Tyler, Ralph Joscelyne and Jacob. Throughout the proceedings the latter was referred to simply by this name. *The Times* reported that Special Branch officers present believed that his surname, Lepidus, was false. The post mortem on Jacob showed a bullet wound on the right temple, about an inch in front of the right ear, on a level with the upper part measuring one inch by about half an inch. There was no sign of singeing or powder-burns. Some bruises on the face had been caused by gunshot, but only one piece of shot had penetrated the skin and that was above the left eye. There was a wound on the right knee, which had not penetrated the joint. Both hands were covered with black powder, particularly the right.

The principal witness was Eagles who, until the inquest, mistakenly believed that he had killed Jacob. But the jury were handed three bullets to inspect – one from Jacob's automatic, one from Eagles' service-revolver, and the bullet which had been extracted from Jacob's head by the doctor. The difference in bullet size made it perfectly clear that Eagles had missed and that Jacob had fired his own gun into his head. The jury's verdict was *felo de se.*

The shootings intensified local feelings against immigrants, particularly Russians. An English shopkeeper in a mainly immigrant area told one newspaper reporter that the foreigners living around his shop were no use to anybody. His complaint has a familiar ring. 'They change their homes every two months. If the guardians relaxed their vigilance for a single week they would go back to their old trick of sleeping twenty-five in a room. Here and there you find a decent, clean man or woman, but nearly all of them are downright riffraff. I have been here a good many years and I have watched this and other roads go down since they infested them.'

Meanwhile, an armed guard was being kept inside and outside the hospital in case Hefeld tried to escape. He was guarded on either side of his bed by an armed policeman. He frequently tried to get up. According to the hospital governor, he would glare around the ward with an expression of terrible ferocity as if maddened by his impotence.

The bullet had entered his head just above the right eye, and for half an inch around the skin was charred. The bullet had passed out of the other side of the forehead lacerating the exit-wound. Although it had passed over the roof of the eye and had caused a fracture, the eye itself had not been injured. There were also some smallshot in the front of the right leg and two pieces of shot in the forehead under the skin.

His wounds closed up and for nearly two weeks he made excellent recovery. But on 9 February it became necessary to operate to remove some pieces of bone at the entrance to the wound which were causing compression of the brain and which had set up meningitis. He died three days later at 9.15 in the evening. Death was due to meningitis caused by laceration and shock. The coroner's jury brought in a verdict of *felo de se*.

While in hospital he had maintained a stubborn silence as to his own identity and history. The only words he is known to have spoken were those at his capture and those he uttered in hospital just before he died.

'My mother is in Riga,' he whispered.

II

Heirs of the Revolution

FROM Tottenham Station, where Tyler's funeral procession entered the High Road, to the cemetery gates is approximately two and a half miles. Stretching from end to end, on either side of the road, stood an unbroken crowd of men and women. Hundreds more watched from windows, balconies and rooftops. For twenty-five minutes the silent crowds gazed at the 3000 policemen walking along behind the coffin, the six plumed horses pulling the hearse and the postilions in black velvet on the backs of the leaders. Tyler's coffin was covered with the Union Jack. So many wreaths had been sent that special carriages had had to be hired to take them to the cemetery. The murdered policeman's widow had sent a white harp of flowers with a broken cord. High-ranking police officers and official government representatives walked in front of the carriages conveying the special mourners.

The same evening the gates of Walthamstow cemetery were locked and the only people present when Jacob was buried were a Baptist minister, the undertaker's men, two policemen and the cemetery superintendent. The coffin bore the words 'Jacob, died January 23, aged about 30'. Three weeks later Paul Hefeld's coffin was lowered into the same unmarked grave. His funeral was by then worth only a cursory paragraph in the newspapers, yet they continued to speculate about the identities of the two men.

'Who are these fiends in human shape, who do not hesitate

to turn their weapons on innocent little boys and harmless women?' the *Daily Mirror* cried. 'The answer is: They are foreign Anarchists, men who have been expelled from Russia for their crimes, whose political creed and religion is that human life is of no value at all.'

After the outbreak of the Japanese war in 1904 large numbers of young Russians, Poles and Letts had escaped abroad to avoid conscription. Many of them settled in Whitechapel and Stepney, and some of the disturbances that took place in their own countries the following year had their genesis in London's East End. 'Blood Sunday' was the signal for the uprising. In Poland, the Ukraine and the Baltic provinces the uprisings were nationalistic and threatened partition. The port of Riga which, in 1905, was the storm centre of the Baltic provinces' revolt against Russian rule was not only the European centre of the timber trade but also the heart of the former state of Latvia. Over the past 400 years it had been fought over and dismembered in turn by Poland, Sweden and Russia, and had remained under Russian domination ever since Peter the Great had at last managed to 'break the window' to the Baltic. In spite of Russification and the emphasis always on Russian culture, language and the Orthodox Church, there had been a slow but gradual revival of national feeling. With the outbreak of revolution in 1905 the Letts saw their chance of freedom at last and made demands for an independent state of Latvia.

Three days after the beginning of the revolt, nearly 15,000 demonstrators marched through the streets of the old town in defiance of a military ban. Some of the demonstrators were armed, and when the troops and police who were waiting to disperse them tried to break them up with rifle-fire they fired back. Some of the demonstrators died in the streets, others on the thin ice as they tried to escape over the partly frozen river. In Riga and elsewhere the uprising was crushed with the utmost brutality. Many young revolutionaries formed underground groups and carried out armed forays to execute *provocateurs* or to rob post offices and government offices. Often they were helped to emigrate or to exist under false identities.

Many of those who had taken part in the revolt escaped abroad. The favourite route was through Libau as this avoided a long railway-journey and a border crossing. It was used chiefly by Jewish émigrés, and the Russian Government turned a blind eye to the port's many irregularities. Similar conditions prevailed at Riga where, the English consul explained, each ship had its recognised quota of stowaways. Ships sailed with '160 passengers who were provided with passports ... more likely about 200 will land in London. The emigrants are supposed to be bound for either the United States of America, or South Africa, and might produce vouchers to this effect, but for a great part these vouchers are blinds and are given gratis by the emigration agents here.'

Most of them settled in the predominantly Jewish East End. Few of them moved nearer to the docks than Cable Street or north beyond the track and goods yards of the Great Eastern Railway. Their boundaries to the east and west were Jubilee Street and the City's Aldgate Pump. Since 1880 many of the worst slums, the old Victorian rookeries of crimes, had been demolished and replaced by new streets and shops, but fewer houses had been built. Despite this, the population had risen from 204 people to an acre, which was the maximum Whitechapel limit, to a new peak of 6000. Immigrant families would squeeze into one or two rooms or into a cellar/kitchen, which often was also a workshop, and sub-let to as many individuals or families as possible. Jewish immigrants quickly adjusted to this new way of life, as they shared the common language of the ghetto; they had their own synagogues, their own schools, their own newspapers and boards of guardians, headed by the great banking families, to help and to advise them. There was nothing comparable for the non-Jewish immigrant, whose ignorance of English disqualified him from any but the most menial jobs.

These political refugees openly carried on their propaganda war. Revolutionary literature was widely circulated in the East End. In one shop a casual passer-by saw and purchased a number of Russian postcards, printed in Whitechapel. One showed the Tsar standing trembling before the headless Louis XIV. Another depicted him as the instigator of the flogging of women, the shooting of old men and the crushing of liberty. The different revolutionary groups met mainly at two clubs: the 'Workers Friend' Club in Jubilee Street, Whitechapel, and the Communist Club in Charlotte Street off the Tottenham Court Road. There were smaller organisations around London, of which those at Tottenham and Edmonton were the strongest. In the provinces the most active centre was probably Liverpool.

After the abortive uprising of 1905 in Russia, the revolutionaries there and abroad resorted once more to partisan tactics, to individual acts of terror, and to the 'expropriation' of state and private funds for party purposes. Travellers in Russia between 1905 and 1908 went in fear of their lives; banks and *bureaux de change* were protected day and night by armed guards. Firearms were subject to very few controls and surprisingly easy to come by. A newspaper noted with astonishment that in December 1905 a Russian bound for London was detained by the Customs at Dover because he was found to have in his luggage forty-seven automatic pistols and nearly 5000 rounds of ammunition. Even more astonishingly he was allowed into the country with his cargo of arms.

'Expropriations' were condemned almost unanimously by the revolutionary leaders. In 1904 the anarchist leader Prince Kropotkin had pleaded, 'Bourgeois money is not necessary for us, either as donations or as thefts', but his words had been widely ignored. In May 1907 the Fifth Congress of the Russian Social Democratic Party, holding their congress in a church in Whitechapel, similarly condemned 'expropriations'. Only the Bolshevik minority voted against the resolution, and it was widely known that their leader, Lenin, depended on 'expropriations' for funds. In June of that year one of the Bolshevik delegates, Stalin, who had shared a room in Whitechapel with Litvinov, the party organiser in Riga smuggling arms into Russia, was heavily implicated in the worst of the Bolshevik 'expropriations' at Tiflis in Georgia.

The Russian authorities could have applied for their extradition, but any attempt to do so would have led to international protests. Russian pogroms and barbaric treatment of political prisoners were a world scandal and one of the reasons why Great Britain had such lenient alien laws. For a long time it was policy not to interfere with foreign political groups as long as they did not use this country as a centre for open propaganda, and it was only occasionally that the police came down heavily on the political refugees.

The *Star* informed its readers on the Monday following the Tottenham shootings that the local anarchists had met in their club room near Ferry Lane; half those present repudiated the two gunmen while the other half had extolled them to the skies. *The Times* corroborated that the membership was almost entirely made up of Letts who worked at two unnamed establishments where, it was said, foreigners were employed in preference to Englishmen. The group was a part of the Lettish Socialistic Revolutionary Party. The Party repudiated the shootings, but did confirm that Jacob and Hefeld had been connected with the local branch, though only through the central finance organisation which was connected with an unnamed Communist club in the West End. In another interview, a member of the Russian Revolutionary Party said that there was no doubt that the two men were members of the Lettish League. He did not think they were anarchists. Probably they were Bolsheviks. However, there could be no doubt that they were criminals before they joined the Revolutionary Party. He had seen Jacob Lepidus at meetings at a Communist club and believed that he was a Russian outlaw.

Further support for these statements came from one man who knew them both, and had been taken to the mortuary to make the identification; subsequently he told a reporter that the police would never find out Jacob's true name although he had been closely linked with the movement in England for about four years. Members, he said, never knew each others' true names. Jacob was a member of the Bolshevik section of the Lettish revolutionaries, but he was not a member of whom they were very proud. He had been a criminal in Russia and had merely joined to cloak acts of robbery. It was thought his family lived near Riga. He was also thought to be the younger brother of Leiser Lepidus, an anarchist, who had been killed two years before in a bomb explosion in Paris on 1 May 1907. Allegedly he was walking along the Bois de Vincennes with a companion when a bomb exploded in his pocket and blew him to pieces. Special Branch officers who went to the inquest on Jacob were apparently convinced that his name was not Jacob Lepidus but, when pressed by reporters for explanations, declined to say why.

Hefeld's identity was equally elusive. The *Daily Mirror* labelled him the emissary of the Anarchist Secret Service corps. His papers showed that he was a sailor, and both men were widely believed to be couriers of anarchist literature, which they had printed in England and smuggled into Russia. So much anarchist literature was found in Hefeld's room that a special car had to be hired to take it away.

In spite of party denials the two men were obviously 'expropriators', but whether for the party or themselves is open to question, although the evidence points strongly towards the former. If this were so, their methods and background were in sharp contrast with their idealism and yet perfectly understandable in the context of their times. A contemporary, writing many years later, explained the problems that faced similar young exiles:

> We had to win our food, lodging and clothing by main force; and after that, to find time to read and think. The problem of the penniless youngster, uprooted or (as we used to say) 'foaming at the bit' through irresistible idealism, confronted us in a form that was practically insoluble. Many comrades were soon to slide into what was called 'illegalism', a way of life not so much on the fringe of society as on the fringe of morality. 'We refuse to be either exploiters or exploited,' they declared, without perceiving that they were continuing to be both these and, what is more, becoming hunted men. When they knew that the game was up they chose to kill themselves rather than go to jail.

One of them, who never went without his Browning revolver, told me, 'Prison isn't worth living for! Six bullets for the sleuth-hounds and the seventh for me!'*

* Victor Serge, *Memoirs of a Revolutionary 1901–1941*.

III

The Expropriators

AMONG those who fled abroad after the 1905 uprising was a young Lithuanian in his early twenties called Jacob Fogel. In common with most exiles he used several aliases; his real name was Jan Sprohe and at some unspecified time in the four years after the 1905 revolution his father had settled in England at Little Witham in Essex. Despite his weak eyes, his vanity for posturing in front of the camera and his slim build, perhaps a legacy from his early years which were spent in utter destitution, Fogel was a dangerous character. There is evidence that he became a militant anarchist and even an active 'expropriator' early in life. In 1905, when he was only sixteen, he was wanted by the police. In the next five years he was wanted for the murder of five men. He had taken part in several bank raids, and on one occasion had been captured but had managed to escape.

In December 1908 or January 1909 he took lodgings in Whitechapel with a comrade called Evan Vanoveitch, nicknamed 'Bifsteks', who was wanted by the Riga police for evading military service. There is inevitably some doubt about his real name. Fogel's arrival marked the beginning of the 'Leesma' or 'Flame' group of Lettish anarchists. A Special Branch report estimated that there were only eight or nine members, but a more reliable source gives the number as fifteen. They had no known meeting-place and none of them were known to any of the recognised groups.

Their landlord was a photographic enlarger, Charles Perelman, who had emigrated from Russia in 1906 together with his wife and family of three sons and three daughters. In the summer of 1908, one of the daughters, Fanny, had met Bifsteks at the Anarchist Club in Jubilee Street. He told her that he was a sailor and employed on a cargo ship to America. He courted her for about six months. During this time he used to visit her home, which was then in Plumbers Row, about once a month when his ship was in dock. When, in the autumn, the family moved to 29 Great Garden Street, a much bigger house as Perelman intended to take in lodgers, Bifsteks came with them and rented the front room on the ground floor. His explanation was that he was on holiday. Two weeks after he moved in, he asked if he could share his room with a friend who was looking for lodgings and introduced the family to 'Grishka Sander', which was one of Fogel's aliases.

The two men were friendly with another lodger, William Sokolow or Sokoloff, but who was better known as Joseph. He was a tall, dark-skinned man with a long thin nose and face, and he walked with a limp. He twisted his body with each step so that his right foot always seemed to be dragging behind his left. Possibly there was some shortening of the leg from an old fracture in the right thigh-bone. By profession he was a watchmaker, but since coming to this country from Russia eleven years before he had worked for twelve different jewellers up and down the country. Except for two long periods of employment his average time had been three to six months with each. In October 1908, soon after he started work as the manager of a jeweller's shop in Old Street, the shop had been burgled. Less than a month later the safe was broken open and jewellery and watches worth about £150 stolen. The police believed that the alleged robbery had been faked, but it was much later before they suspected that he had probably organised it with Fogel and Bifsteks.

When, three months later, the Tottenham robbery was committed less than six miles away, Fogel, who seems to have been under observation of some kind by the Special Branch, was im-

mediately suspected of being implicated. None of the money
had been recovered, and it was widely believed that it had been
passed to a third accomplice in the early stages of the chase when
this would have been possible. The police were convinced that
Fogel was the third man but they had no proof. The strain was
too much for their landlord, who evidently realised the police
suspicions, and he ordered Bifsteks as well as Fogel to leave.
Before they went they shared their room for one night with a
fellow Lett, a young locksmith recently returned from America
and who was also wanted by the Riga police, called Fritz Svaars.
Next day Svaars rented the room on the floor above them.

Fritz Svaars was 22–5 years old. He spoke English and
German imperfectly. He was square-shouldered with light-
brown hair and a turned-up moustache which partly concealed
the few small pimples or smallpox scars on his face. His eyes
were grey, and he hunched his shoulders slightly when he
walked. His clothes were American style and normally he wore
a thin-striped brown-tweed suit, a dark melton overcoat with a
velvet collar, and either a grey Irish-tweed cap with red spots or
a trilby. In October 1905 he had been arrested in Riga with
four others on suspicion of tearing down telephone wires, rob-
bing two state-owned shops and the administration offices at
Pormsaten, killing a policeman and killing also the keeper of a
state-owned shop at Oberbartovo. On 16 October the five
suspects had managed to escape from their place of detention
at Grabin; but three months later, in January 1906, Fritz was
recaptured in Riga where he was living under the assumed
name of Karl Davidoff Dumnek. After some days in captivity
he successfully escaped again and this time disappeared for
three years. Except for his cousin's statements that Fritz at some
time in 1906 was a sailor, nothing positive is known about him
until his appearance at 29 Great Garden Street.

He was joined in the next two weeks by Mouremtzoff, alias
George Gardstein. They shared the room for the next three
months. Both men, like Fogel, were wanted for expropriations.
Fritz was wanted for a bank raid in Pennsylvania where a
reward of $2000 was being offered, Gardstein for a similar

robbery in Germany. Soon there was a regular flow of visitors to the house. Names were kept to a minimum and frequently the visitors were only known by their Christian names or nicknames. Regular visitors were Yourka Dubof, Karl Hoffman and John Rosen, whose physical resemblance to Fritz was so startling that they were mistakenly thought by several people who knew them to be brothers. Fritz's only relation, in fact, was his cousin Jacob Peters who arrived in London in July or October 1909 from Riga. He was an active member of the Lettish Social Democratic Party and for seven years had carried out propaganda work in the Army and in the docks. Following the 1905 uprising he had been imprisoned for eighteen months and tortured. His fingers were scarred where the nails had been torn out. Prison had only made him stronger, and he was fanatically devoted to the overthrow of the Tsarist state. He mistakenly thought that Fritz's fanaticism was equal to his own, and was disappointed to find that the old enthusiasm was not there but had been replaced by lukewarm anarchism. They soon quarrelled, and Peters moved into other lodgings.

The back room of 29 Great Garden Street was rented to a young woman named Nina Vassilleva. She became Gardstein's mistress. For a time she was extremely close to their landlord's family, particularly Fanny Perelman, who presented her with a group photograph of herself, her father and Gardstein, and inscribed it 'To dear Nina from the "wicked" Fenia'. Their friendship lasted until February/March 1910 when they fell out, and Charles Perelman ordered Nina to leave his lodging-house at 74 Wellesley Street where he had moved a few months previously. He was also renting a room to Yourka Dubof. But several months prior to this move he had given Gardstein and Fritz notice to quit and used the actual move itself as an excuse for also getting rid of Joseph with whom they had a close friendship.

Gardstein moved to 44 Gold Street and rented a back room in the name of P. Morin. In March 1910, the tenancy changed hands. The new landlord was an Austrian Jew, a boot-clicker named Jacob Kempler. Kempler agreed to keep him on as a lodger at four shillings a week but he was puzzled by Gardstein's long, unexplained absences. From the quantity of laboratory equipment and chemicals in his room, he thought he was a chemist. Gardstein encouraged this belief and always asked that the door of his room, when he was away for any length of time, should be kept locked. The only key he possessed was in fact for the street door. He disappeared twice in 1910, between May and July, and from September to the middle of October, taking with him only a small portmanteau and promising to pay the rent when he returned. The first time he went away Joseph came to Gold Street with a letter from him saying that he could sleep in his room in his absence. He stayed for five weeks until the landlord became exasperated by the amount of rent owing and ordered him out.

Fritz Svaars disappeared for almost a year. At some time he returned to Riga, and in January 1910 he was captured by the Russian Secret Police. He managed to keep his identity hidden but in the eleven days he was in police hands he received so many beatings that his head felt quite soft, he later wrote to his sister Lisa. He was released on bail but followed everywhere he went. Eventually he managed to give his followers the slip and escape abroad once more. But the beatings had apparently broken his spirit, and when he returned to England in June 1910 he had made up his mind to send for his wife, who was still living in the Baltic, and emigrate to Australia.

For the next five months much of his limited social life centred on the Anarchist Club in Jubilee Street. Formerly it had been a Salvation Army depot but in 1906 it had been opened as a working men's institute by Prince Kropotkin. The building had two large halls, one on the ground floor, and another on the second floor containing a library, reading-room and classrooms. It was an international meeting-place for anarchists but open to all workers of whatever political creed. It was here, through Gardstein, who had introduced her to the club, that Fritz met Luba Milstein; they soon became lovers. They had a stormy relationship. In the first month they quarrelled so fiercely that Fritz left her without saying where he was going and disappeared for two weeks. When he returned he was in possession of several watches apparently part of the proceeds of an 'expropriation'. He gave one to Luba and kept the others for pawning. Certainly she must have suspected what he was doing but this was not the cause of their quarrelling, which continued for the whole of their relationship. He told her bluntly that he was a married man and planning to emigrate to Australia with his wife. Certainly these facts were well known to even casual acquaintances.

But Luba was so besotted with Fritz that, as she later wrote, if he had told her at midday that it was midnight she would have believed him. Fritz found lodgings at 35 Newcastle Place and rented the single room on the first floor from the landlord, Abraham Smolensky, a Hebrew teacher, who lived in the two rooms below, and Luba moved in with him. Her father, a commission agent, had died in Russia four years before, but her family were living at 2 Cecil Street off the Mile End Road. Her brother Jack had a tailor's shop in Branch Yard, White-chapel, and she worked for him as a skirt hand twelve hours a day with an hour's break for lunch. Normally she finished at 8 p.m., but sometimes sooner if the work was slack. Jack, and another brother Nathan, soon discovered that she was living with a married man but they could not discover from her where they lived. In spite of the family nagging, she continued to work at Branch Yard. The only stabilising influence in her life at this point was her friendship with another skirt hand employed by her brother, a small hunchbacked woman called Sara Rosa Trassjonsky.

Luba was passionately in love with Fritz but it is doubtful whether he returned her affection. Her presence did not deter him from sharing their one room with his friends. Gardstein, Karl Hoffman and John Rosen were regular visitors; and for five weeks, until they moved for the last time to 59 Grove Street, the room was used daily by Peter Piaktow alias Peter Schtern but better known as Peter the Painter, who had recently arrived from Paris. It is extremely doubtful whether Schtern or Piatkow was his real name, but it is known that he was from Pskow in the Courland Province. Like others in the group he had been imprisoned for acts committed in the revolution of 1905, but had escaped and hidden in his birthplace with some friends, and earned a living painting street doors and numbers. His father died in 1908 but his mother and sisters still lived at their farm somewhere near Talsen. He had travelled widely in Europe. While living in Marseilles, an uncle, who was an army colonel, told him that if he would go to Paris and study – anything but politics – he would send him money each month. This offer was apparently rejected, and Piaktow continued to earn his living as a house painter. He liked working hard and in Marseilles used to earn a fair living. He was a vegetarian, but enjoyed smoking and playing cards. He had a girl friend, Anna Schwarz, in Russia. At night he slept in Karl Hoffman's lodgings at 36 Lindley Street.

On 4 November Fritz and Luba, with Peter, moved to 59 Grove Street, to two first-floor rooms found for them by old Mr Reuben, the grocer, Smolensky later said that he gave them notice because of the number of their visitors – ten to twelve at a time – the mandoline-playing and the late hours; according to Luba they moved because Fritz and Peter did not want to be separated. Either explanation could be true. Gardstein helped them to bundle their few possessions onto a coster's barrow. Peter took possession of the front room, though it was bigger than the back room which Fritz and Luba kept for themselves, and despite the fact that they paid the rent for both.

Soon there was the usual run of visitors; Gardstein, Joseph, Hoffman, Rosen and a newcomer Max Smoller, whom Luba had seen loitering about Reuben's grocery. Luba knew Fritz was a locksmith, but living with him – and as work slackened off at the tailor's shop she spent more and more time at home – she began to realise that Fritz had little, if any, regular employment. The same was true of Peter the Painter, although Fritz told her that he was studying art and that his parents were sending him money. (His poverty and total dependence on Fritz indicates that his uncle was not.) She asked Fritz how he earned his money but he told her curtly to mind her own business. She must have guessed. She knew that Fritz occasionally carried a Browning, and Gardstein the less compact but more deadly Mauser which he concealed in a specially constructed trouser pocket. She knew nothing of the group and began to resent their presence. She had no keys, not even to the street door, and often she was excluded from the meetings in the front room, which were never explained to her; conversations were whispered or switched into another language, which she did not understand, if she came near. Occasionally she was allowed into the front room but at other times, coming home weary from work and worried by the persistent nagging of her brothers, she would scream at the constant noise and muddle, and humiliate Fritz in front of the others. Worse still was the knowledge that Fritz had sent money to his wife, who would be joining him in January 1911.

Her behaviour was an added reason why Nina Vassilleva and Jacob Peters stayed away. Fritz did not particularly like Gardstein's mistress, and she never visited his new lodgings, although Gardstein was a daily visitor. Peters only came a few times, but it was their political differences basically that kept the cousins apart. Only Gardstein held the group together and, in Fogel's absence, he assumed the leadership. Fogel, if he were needed, could still be contacted through Bifsteks' fiancée, Fanny Perelman, or through Karl Hoffman whom he apparently saw on rare occasions. Gardstein was the obvious choice as leader, particularly as Fritz was still suffering from broken nerves and planned to emigrate. The group's future plans did not include Fritz.

As usual, the information for the next expropriation came from Joseph. He had once worked for a jeweller in Houndsditch in the city of London and he now heard that since May a new shop 'H. S. Harris' had opened which was reputed to be the wealthiest in the street. Access would have to be from one of the empty houses in Exchange Buildings, behind the shop, which would have to be rented. Cutting equipment would also have to be bought to open the large iron safe that was visible from the street. But the group's finances were parlously low.

It was possibly on the understanding that he would provide the finance that Joseph introduced Max Smoller to the group.

Smoller lived with his wife and two children in Wellesley Street, not far from Perelman's lodging-house. According to Nina Vassilleva, he and Joseph had once been caught and tried for a fur robbery in which they were both implicated. They were great friends still – in fact, Joseph had such great admiration for Max that he boasted that he was his pupil. Both men were said to be wanted in the Crimea for a number of jewel robberies similar to the one they were now planning. If Max was providing the finance, which could only have been a few pounds, Gardstein was providing the men, and some sort of challenge for the leadership developed between them – enough to make Nina frightened for her lover's safety.

The houses in Exchange Buildings, a cul-de-sac at the back of Houndsditch, were owned by Millard Brothers in Houndsditch. On 21 November a pimply faced man with thick lips and the appearance of an East European Jew called at the office to ask whether they had any houses to let, as he was in business in the West End and he wanted somewhere handy for himself and his wife. He spoke fairly good English and said that his name was Joe Levi; in reality it was Max Smoller. He said that he was anxious to move in quickly; but two or three days later, when he called back to ask if the house was ready, he was told that a better one, No. 11, would be vacant by the end of the week. Having looked over it he said that he would take it as it did not need so much doing-up. His rent was ten shillings a week, and he took possession on 2 December.

The hesitation over the choice of house is understandable as No. 10, which backed on to the jewellers, had already been let. The exact position of the shop was uncertain. The back yards were only three feet wide and the view was obscured by a wall which was higher than the houses. No. 9 was still empty but to rent that too was beyond the gang's means at that time.

Gardstein's plans had not included Fritz, but now he had to be brought in. Money was also needed for extra equipment. He asked Fritz to lend him 100 roubles (£10) for two weeks.

Fritz had already spent 160 roubles on his boat tickets to
Australia and sent 100 roubles to his wife to join him; he could
only manage 60 roubles, which left him a meagre 20 roubles
(£2) in cash. He gave Gardstein the last watches he had kept
for pawning from the last expropriation, and even took back
from Luba the watch he had given her to raise the extra money.
After several months of boring inactivity and domestic
squabbles it was not too difficult for Gardstein to persuade him
to take part in the expropriation, although Fritz's experiences
earlier in the year had made him terrified of being caught. On
6 December, Fritz, using the name Goldstein, speaking broken
English and carrying an umbrella, rented No. 9 Exchange
Buildings. He explained that he only wanted it for two or three
weeks to store Christmas goods and paid five shillings deposit.
He took possession on 12 December. Gardstein, meanwhile,
used some of the money borrowed to buy a large quantity of
chemicals, a book on brazing metals and cutting metals with
acid.

Most of the inhabitants of the other houses in Exchange
Buildings assumed that the new tenants were a newly married
couple and wished to be left alone. Occasionally they saw Nina
Vassilleva in a white blouse and blue skirt taking down the
shutters or walking out of No. 11 with a shawl pulled over her
face. Max and Joseph, who stayed with her, were rarely seen;
they slept in the first-floor bedroom and Nina on the sofa downstairs. Their furniture was borrowed from Fritz and Gardstein.
Luba's reaction – she still did not know what was happening –
can easily be guessed.

Now they had the two houses the only obstacle in their way
was the occupied house in between directly backing onto the
shop. It had been rented by a Rumanian, Michail Silisteanu.
He was an ex-journalist who for the past three years had been
trying to interest the British public in a game he had patented
called 'Flyscout'. He occupied only the top room of the house
which contained a bed, table and chairs and a large quantity
of cardboard boxes. Fortunately for the group's plans the police
intervened and brought an unexpected solution to their problem.

Silisteanu's office was in 73 St Mary Axe near by, and he hired girls to demonstrate his game in the window. When crowds started to block the pavement there was the inevitable brush with the law. The police told him that the City's bye-laws empowered them to stop the demonstration. Nor would they allow him to give out handbills. Silisteanu left for Paris in disgust on 12 December. The owners, Millard Brothers, used No. 10 temporarily for storing goods but planned to take the last of them out by Friday, 16 December.

Gardstein organised the final details of the robbery, including the purchase of a cylinder of oxygen, and a final briefing was held in Fritz's lodgings on the afternoon of 16 December. The only people absent were Nina Vassilleva, who was already at Exchange Buildings, and Jacob Peters, who had arranged to go directly to the house later that evening.

Gardstein counted on thirty-six hours at the most in which to break into the shop and rob the safe. Apart from the rear wall adjoining No. 10, a second wall had to be broken behind the safe, which then had to be cut open from behind; it was in full view of anyone who happened to look through the shop window, including the policeman on his beat. Obviously it was likely to be a lengthy business and they might have to work through two nights and a day. Those taking part were split into two groups. In the first was Gardstein himself, Max Smoller, Jacob Peters and Yourka Dubof. The last named was one of the gang's three locksmiths and was a logical inclusion in case they broke through sooner than expected. The other two locksmiths were Fritz and Osip Federoff.

Fritz and Joseph were in the second group. They were both bad risks to take on the initial breakthrough. Fritz's fear of being caught made him a bad risk at any time, and Joseph's lame leg was likely to stop him escaping if anything went wrong. The others on stand-by were Karl Hoffman in 36 Lindley Street, Osip Federoff (it is not known where he was) and John Rosen, who later told his fiancée that if anyone had gone sick he was the next to be called.

Clearly there had to be a prearranged meeting-place in case

anything did go wrong, and Fritz's lodgings were a natural choice. The others either lived in rooms which they shared with strangers, or in rooms which were too far away or totally unsuitable for their purpose. Besides, Fritz's landlord was accustomed to his late hours and the comings and goings of his friends. The only problem was Luba. Fortunately she would never go into the front room if she knew that anyone was there, and it was a simple matter to arrange for Peter the Painter, who was only a bystander to the robbery, to be there and keep her out. Both doors opened onto the landing and unlit staircase, and there was no connecting door between the rooms. Because Peter would be covering for them, Fritz could hide there unknown to Luba and Joseph wait with him. (See below, page 79.)

The initial breakthrough did not begin until after 7 p.m., which was the time Millard Brothers took the last of their Christmas stock out of No. 10 and locked the door. In the darkness the men scrambled over the lavatory roof from the yard of No. 11 and soon began to hammer away at the lavatory wall, which was also the back wall of Harris's shop. The noise, since it could be heard in the shops in Houndsditch, must have sounded even more exaggerated to the men making it and Dubof, whose sensitive fingers might be needed for the safe, went outside and wandered about the adjoining streets, in Cutler Street and Houndsditch, to see if there was any reaction to the noise and, if the police were called, to give the others warning to get out. But it was the eve of the Jewish Sabbath and the streets were almost deserted.

IV

The House with
Green Shutters

LATE Friday evening, 16 December 1910, there was a high
wind blowing through Houndsditch. Gas lamps flickered, and
the streets were deserted. The street was all that was left of the
protective moat or ditch that used to run outside the City wall
from the Tower of London, in the east, to Blackfriars in the
west, and which at one time stretched as far north as Moorgate
and Cripplegate. It was called Houndsditch, or Dogditch, because the Common Hunt used to fling into it the carcases of
the dogs he slaughtered and which were believed in the sixteenth and seventeenth centuries to carry the plague. Gradually
the ditch had been built over until all that was left was a strip
running north to south from Bishopsgate to Aldgate. At the
northern tip was the church of St Botolph-without-Bishopsgate
and at the southern end the church of St Botolph, Aldgate. Outside the church prostitutes solicited for customers – they kept
within the law by never stopping but walking all the time
around the surrounding piece of burial ground; inside the
church, in a glass case, was the mummified head of the Tudor
Duke of Suffolk, severed on Tower Hill. In Mitre Square near
by the locals would point to Ripper's Corner where in the
autumn of 1888 Jack the Ripper disembowelled one of his
victims.

Max Weil closed his shop door and, stepping out into the

street, peered through the window of the shop next door. The centre of the window was empty except for the velvet-covered shelves displaying on either side ornaments and scattered bric-à-brac. High up, in the centre of the window, was a large ornate clock, with a case shaped like the Eiffel Tower partly masked by the words 'ESTD 1865' on the window.

The overhead sign creaking in the wind and projecting from the first-floor window read 'No. 119 H. S. Harris. Jewellers from 1865'. This particular shop had only been open since May and old man Harris had left the management of it to his son Harry. The bostwick gate was locked and there was an observation light burning in the inner office. Peering through the window, Weil could see the office door open, flat against the wall, and in the corner, under the light, a jeweller's heavy iron safe. Everything appeared to be in order and yet Weil felt uneasy. He lived next door in a flat over his fancy-goods business with his sister and their maidservant, Edith Chard. He had been out until about 10 p.m., and when he returned home had found the two women agitated by unusual noises coming from downstairs at the back of the shop. Weil had immediately gone down to his counting-house, where the noises seemed to be coming from, but finding nothing wrong had gone into the street to see if anyone was still working in the jewellers. Finding nobody, he thought he had better report the matter to the police. If people were trying to break in they would have nearly thirty-six hours in which to do so; next day was Saturday, the Jewish Sabbath, and the shop would stay closed. Besides, he too had heard the rumours about the Tsarist crown-jewels.

In Bishopsgate he found a young City constable, Walter Piper, who followed him back. Together they listened to the noises for a while and both agreed that they sounded like the 'drilling, sawing and breaking away of brickwork'. Piper thought there was probably some innocent explanation but went to the back – to the small cul-de-sac, Exchange Buildings – to investigate. The lights were on in the Cutlers Arms on the north-east corner and he knocked on the door immediately opposite, which was No. 12. He asked if anyone was working in the yard at the back and, drawing a blank, he moved on to the next house and knocked again.

The ground floor of No. 11 Exchange Buildings had an old-fashioned folding shop-front and each of its three windows was covered by a green shutter except for a gap of about six inches at the top through which the gaslight was gleaming. The door was opened so quickly, and the manner of the man who opened it was so furtive, that Piper's suspicions were immediately aroused. Instead of repeating his question and arousing the man's suspicions, he said the first thing that came into his head: 'Is the missus in?'

Gardstein shook his head. 'She has gone out.'

Piper shrugged indifferently. 'Right, I will call back,' he said and walked away.

When he heard the door close behind him he tapped lightly once more on the door of No. 12. 'How far is Harris's from here?' he asked. He went through into the narrow yard at the back and tried to judge for himself; then he left. As he walked towards Cutler Street he could see a man lurking in the shadows at the entrance of the cul-de-sac watching him. He approached the man, who walked away; there was something about the way he walked that made Piper feel he could identify him if he saw him again.

In Houndsditch Piper saw two constables from adjoining beats, Walter Choat and Ernest Woodhams. He told them of Weil's suspicions but not that he had been to Exchange Buildings or that he had spoken to Gardstein and so put the gang on their guard. Choat stopped in Houndsditch to watch the front of the jeweller's shop and Woodhams placed himself at the entrance to the cul-de-sac, while Piper went back to Bishopsgate Police Station for help. Nobody could get in or out of the buildings without being seen by either of the two policemen. On his way into the station, which was only a few minutes' walk, Piper met one of the duty sergeants, Robert Bentley, and two plain-clothes constables, James Martin and Arthur Strongman. Strongman was sent back to the station with a message for the Night Duty Inspector to telephone Harris and ask him to come and open his shop.

Weil took Bentley through to his counting-house to listen. As they were talking the hammering stopped and there was some conjecture later as to whether their voices had been heard through the none-too-thick wall. By now, other people had also heard the hammering and had become alarmed. Mrs Jones and her daughter, at the dairy shop on the other side of Harris's, saw the policemen waiting outside the shop and told them what they had heard. Strongman was waiting outside with two sergeants, Bryant and Tucker (affectionately known as 'Daddy'), and Constable Smoothey, and had a message for Bentley from Chief Inspector Hayes. Hayes was suspicious of some foreigners living on the right-hand side of the Exchange Buildings where the noises were coming from; Bentley was to find out if they were making the noise.

Piper was only a probationer constable and he was ordered to take Choat's place in front of Harris's shop out of harm's way. Constable Smoothey was positioned at the corner of Houndsditch and Cutler Street, and Woodhams was left where he was, at the entrance to the cul-de-sac. In this way there was a connecting chain between the two points and instant communication. Bentley went with the others to No. 11 Exchange Buildings. None of them knew that Piper had been to the house fifteen minutes previously. The time was now about 11.30 p.m.

Bentley knocked on the door of No. 11 and slowly the bar of light on the pavement outside widened as the door was pulled back. 'Have you been working or knocking about inside?' he asked. Gardstein peered at the policeman suspiciously and ignored the question. 'Don't you understand English?' Still there was no answer. 'Have you got anybody in the house that can?' persisted the sergeant. 'Fetch them down.' Gardstein pushed the door partly to. Constable Martin who was standing outside guessed that he had gone upstairs, as he could see into the room and Gardstein did not cross his line of vision.

Almost directly opposite, at No. 5, sixteen-year-old Bessie Jacobs peeped through the door to see what was happening. In spite of the heavy winter-greatcoats and the combed helmets she instantly recognised the burly figure of Constable Choat. 'Hello missie,' he said. Bessie opened the door a little wider.

'Nice to see you after all this time,' she called out.

Choat ignored the implied question. His mother had just died and he had been at home in the country settling her affairs. He nodded towards the partly open door. 'We've got a little something we have to do.' Bessie's mother called downstairs and asked what was happening. She was ill in bed with pneumonia and her daughter was supposed to be making coffee and fetching coal for the bedroom fire. Bessie left the door partly ajar. As she went inside she heard one of the policemen further down the cul-de-sac, who could not see what was happening, growl, 'Open the door or we're going to smash it in.' His words must have carried. At the same time the lights in the Cutlers Arms were turned off.

Bentley pushed open the door of No. 11. There was no connecting door between the small lobby at the foot of the stairs and the room on his right. There was a large fire burning in the grate and on the table were three cups and saucers, but otherwise the room was empty. Sergeant Bryant stepped into the doorway behind him for a closer look. Suddenly both men realised that they were being watched from the stairs. They could not see the man's face because the stairs were very dark, only the bottom of his trouser legs.

'Is anybody working here?' Bentley asked.

'No.'

'Anyone in the back?'

'No.'

'Can I have a look in the back?'

'Yes.'

'Show us the way.'

The man on the stairs pointed to the room and spoke for the last time.

'In there,' he said.

Bentley stepped further into the room. As he did so the back
door was flung open and a man, mistakenly identified as Gardstein, walked rapidly into the room. He was holding a pistol
which he fired as he advanced with the barrel pointing towards
the unarmed Bentley. As he opened fire so did the man on the
stairs. The shot fired from the stairs went through the rim of
Bentley's helmet, across his face and out through the shutter behind him. 'Gardstein' by now had closed to within three or four
feet and was firing just across the table. At point-blank range he
could not miss. His first shot hit Bentley in the shoulder and the
second went through his neck almost severing his spinal cord.
Bentley staggered back against the half-open door and collapsed backwards over the doorstep so that he was lying half in
and half out of the house. Bryant, who had been standing partly
behind him, glimpsed the pistol turning towards him and put
out his hands instinctively, as he said later, 'to ward off the
flashes'. He felt his left hand fall to his side and then, stumbling
over the dying Bentley, he fell into the street. He had only a
hazy recollection of what followed but he remembered getting
up and staggering along the pavement. Fortunately he walked
away from the entrance to the cul-de-sac, which probably saved
his life. He was very dazed and fell down again. He regained
consciousness some minutes later and found himself propped up
against the wall of one of the houses. He had been shot in the
arm and slightly wounded in the chest.

Constable Woodhams saw Bentley fall backwards over the
doorstep and ran to help him. He could not see who was doing
the shooting. Suddenly his leg buckled beneath him as a
Mauser bullet shattered his thigh bone and he fell unconscious
to the ground. Constable Strongman and Sergeant Tucker saw
him fall but neither could see who was doing the shooting. Only
a hand clutching a pistol protruded from the doorway. 'The
hand was followed by a man aged about 30, height 5 ft 6 or 7,
pale thin face, dark curly hair and dark moustache, dress dark
jacket suit, no hat, who pointed the revolver in the direction
of Sergeant Tucker and myself, firing rapidly. P. S. Tucker
and I stepped back a few yards, when the sergeant staggered

and turned round.' Strongman caught him by the arm and Tucker staggered the length of the cul-de-sac before collapsing in the roadway. He had been shot twice, once in the hip and once in the heart. He died almost instantly.

Martin, who like Strongman was in plain clothes, had been standing by the open door when the shooting started. As Bentley then Bryant staggered back bleeding from gun wounds, he turned and ran for the partly open door behind him. Bessie Jacobs' first thought when she heard the opening shots was that the high wind had blown the chimney pot off. But then she saw the gun flashes through the tops of the shutters. She pulled her nightclothes tighter round her and as she reached the door it burst open and Martin leaped inside. He slammed the door behind him as she began to scream. He covered her mouth with his hand. 'Don't scream, I'm a detective,' he pleaded. 'I'll protect your mother and I'll protect you.'

In the darkness, some of the targets were little more than shadows, and bullets splintered and gouged the wooden fronts of the houses as the gang raced for the entrance. Twenty-two shots were fired. Gardstein had almost reached the entrance when Constable Choat caught hold of him by the wrist and fought him for possession of his gun. As Gardstein pulled the trigger repeatedly Choat desperately pushed the pistol away from the centre of his body and the shots were fired into his left leg. Others of the gang rushed to Gardstein's assistance and turned their guns on Choat. He was a big, muscular man, 6 feet 4 inches tall, and in spite of the darkness a target impossible to miss. He was shot five more times. The last two bullets were fired into his back. As he fell backwards he dragged Gardstein with him and a shot, fired at Choat, hit Gardstein in the back. Choat was kicked in the face to make him release his grip on Gardstein, who was seized by two of the group and dragged away. But already he was a dying man.

When the shooting stopped, the dazed inhabitants came out of their houses. In No. 12 Mr Abrahams muttered that he knew that there was something up and blew a whistle as his fourteen-year-old son ran outside in time to see Sergeant Tucker die in the arms of Harry Jacobs, the second-hand-clothes dealer. His mother had hysterics, ran screaming out of the house and fell over one of the bodies. The door of No. 5 opened cautiously and Constable Martin slipped outside after begging Bessie Jacobs to promise not to say anything. Almost the first thing they saw was the shattered figure of Constable Choat struggling up on his hands and knees for just a few seconds before collapsing; in spite of his terrible wounds he was, however, still alive. Martin went over to the dying Bentley still sprawled in the doorway and when he saw the wound in his neck unbuttoned his tunic. He was helped by a young tailor's-presser, Sam Hart, who lived in Artizan Street. Like most people who heard them, he had thought at first that the shots were chimney pots blowing down in the wind. As he ran through Harrow Alley he had seen two men coming towards him, dragging what he thought was a drunk between them. There was a woman walking behind them and when she saw him running she had screamed, 'Go back, go back.' Hart had only run faster and it was not until later that he realised that the 'drunk' was Gardstein and the escaping gang. In Exchange Buildings he saw Bentley sprawled in the gaslight, lying with his head and shoulders on the pavement. Hart helped Martin do what he could for Bentley and then turned his attention to Bryant, who was walking about in a state of shock. He sat him down, propped him up against a wall and undid his tunic. For some unexplained reason, Hart thought that the police had been shot while raiding a gambling den.

Constable Piper, who had been in Houndsditch when the shooting started, ran to Cutler Street and saw Sergeant Tucker fall to the ground – a minute or two at the most after he had been shot, according to the doctor. He ran back to Houndsditch, stopped a motor-car, bundled the passengers out and sent Constable Smoothey with Sergeant Tucker to the London Hospital. Tucker was already dead when he was examined by Dr Rainey in the Receiving room at about 11.50 p.m. His tunic was open and the third button from the top had had a piece taken out of its edge. There was a small puncture wound two inches from the centre of the body, right over the position of the heart. This was the bullet that had killed him. There was a second bullet wound in the left lateral line of the body, four inches above the hip bone.

Dr Rainey had just finished his examination when Constable Choat was brought in on a stretcher. He was obviously suffering from shock and loss of blood and was immediately taken to the wards. He was conscious but had no memory of what had happened. His mouth, nose and eyes were bruised, which could have been caused by a fall or a blow. There were eight bullet wounds. The first was just above the spine of the right scapula; the second an inch to the right of the tenth dorsal spine; the third in the left loin an inch below the tip of the tenth rib, which was larger and more lacerated than the other wounds; the fourth and fifth were in the left thigh, one on the outside and one on the inside; the sixth, seventh and eighth were in the right calf, the outer side of the right foot by the toe and on the inner side about centre. He did not feel any pain. He was not losing blood externally but he was obviously suffering from haemorrhage and the rupture of some hollow organ. Some fluid was injected in the veins of his arms. He was operated on immediately. An incision was made in the right side of his abdomen and a ragged fragment of bullet was found just beneath the skin. Three feet of the upper part of the small intestine was found to be lacerated in five places; that piece was removed. He was too ill to withstand further surgery. He was taken back to the ward where he died two hours later, at 5.20 a.m., Saturday, 17 December 1910.

Bentley was carried to St Bartholemew's Hospital where he arrived just before midnight. He was suffering from cerebral irritation and was struggling and calling out. He was only semi-conscious when he was examined. There were two bullet wounds, one in front of the right shoulder-joint and one in the neck. The spinal cord had been partly severed and by morning his lower limbs were paralysed. He regained consciousness at some time during the day and was able to answer quite rationally the questions put to him, and he probably spoke to his

wife, who was expecting a baby. At 6.45 p.m. his breathing
became more difficult and his condition worsened rapidly. He
died forty-five minutes later.

Within minutes of the shooting policemen were rushed from
Bishopsgate Police Station to Exchange Buildings. In the early
hours they were hampered by the lack of information. Bryant
had wandered away, still in a daze and clutching his arm, to
find a doctor, and the only other witnesses to the shootings were
Woodhams, who was still unconscious from the crippling shot
to his leg, Strongman who had caught the dying Tucker and
helped him away, and Martin, who reported untruthfully that
he had not seen anything because he had stumbled and fallen.
Piper had come into Cutler Street from the Houndsditch end
and must have realised that the wanted men could only have
gone out through Harrow Alley, but was busy sending the dead
and wounded men away to hospital and raising the alarm.
There was no way of passing this information on. The only
police-box system in use at the time was an ambulance call-box.
Anyone could communicate with the headquarters telephone-
room simply by lifting the receiver, but there was no flashing
light or other signal by which the telephone room could get in
touch with them. Messages had to be passed on by foot or by
pedal-cycle. The only mechanised transport the police possessed
was an electric ambulance.

Shortly before midnight Detective Superintendent John Ottaway took charge. Like the detectives with him he was armed.
Possible witnesses were taken into the Cutlers Arms – where
the fact that the police never paid for the brandy that was
consumed that night was remembered for years afterwards
– and the cul-de-sac was sealed off. At the blind end a large
quantity of timber planking was stacked against the warehouse
wall, and this was thoroughly searched in case any member
of the gang had been unable to get away and had hidden
there. After Bentley had been carried out of the doorway, the
door of No. 11 had been left open and watery gaslight was
still flickering over the pavement when the first detectives
entered the house. The fire was banked up. On the table was a

cup of freshly made tea, some bread, paste, jam and sardines, together with a pressure gauge, a double blowpipe fitted with seven feet of flexible metallic tubing, a similar length of rubber tubing and two stop-cocks. There was a clutter of chairs in the room and a gas stove; on the floor were pieces of oil cloth. The most distinctive piece of furniture was a chest-of-drawers belonging to Fritz.

Two panes of glass had been broken in the window by the door, one apparently from a bullet fired from the stairs. There were also two bullet holes in the ceiling, so that it looked as if one of the men had paused by the door and fired two warning shots into the air. One of the bullets had gone through the ceiling and lodged in the ceiling of the first floor bedroom which was the only one of the two upstairs rooms, one above the other, which had been used. White lace and green-cloth curtains covered the windows, and on the black and brass bedstead were two red feather-pillows and a plaid quilt.

The back door led into a small yard about fourteen feet long by three feet wide with a sink at one end and a lavatory at the other. There were marks on the wall and pipe near the sink where somebody had scrambled over into No. 10, which was empty. Again there were signs that somebody had climbed from there into the next-door house, over the wall into No. 9. In the yard was a cylinder containing forty feet of oxygen-compressed gas; broken bricks littered the ground and blocked the lavatory pan. The seat was covered with brown paper on which were diamond-pointed drills, a carpenter's brace, chisel, crowbars and a special wrench with jagged jaws, similar to a tin opener, for ripping metal. In the wall, reaching through to the matchwood at the back of Harris's shop, a gaping hole had been torn in the brickwork, 24 inches high by 20 inches across and 9 inches deep. In the house was 60 feet of rubber tubing, fixed to the gas pipe, some mortar, wax candles, sand and asbestos boards. The bolt working the street-door handle had been fastened back with a screw so that the door could only be opened with a key.

The robbery would have been possible, but only just. The

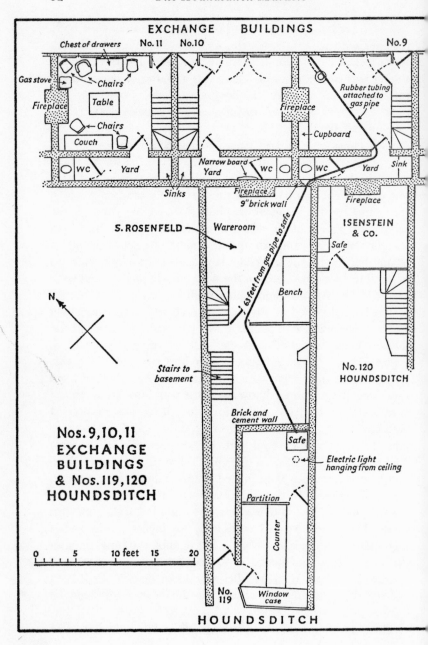

EXCHANGE BUILDINGS

Chest of drawers No. 11 No. 10 No. 9

Gas stove

Chairs

Fireplace

Table

Chairs

Couch

Rubber tubing
attached to
gas pipe

Fireplace

←Cupboard

WC · Yard

Narrow board
Yard WC WC Yard Sink

Sinks

Fireplace
9" brick wall

S. ROSENFELD Wareroom

ISENSTEIN
& CO.

Safe

63 feet from gas pipe to safe

Bench

N

Stairs to
basement

No. 120
HOUNDSDITCH

Brick and
cement wall

Nos. 9, 10, 11
EXCHANGE
BUILDINGS
& Nos. 119, 120
HOUNDSDITCH

Safe

Electric light
hanging from ceiling

Partition

Counter

0 5 10 feet 15 20

No.
119

Window
case

HOUNDSDITCH

distance to the safe was 60 feet and the tubing was 63, which would have only given them a clearance of 3 feet to the back of the safe.

The night's most important witness was fourteen-year-old Solomon Abrahams, who lived next door at No. 12, and who claimed to have seen the killings. He stated he was standing by the door when he

> heard a smash of glass at No. 11. A man then opened the door, I did not see his face, I only saw his arm and heard a report of a firearm and immediately saw the policeman fall into the doorway. A man then ran out of the door with a revolver in his hand and fired about eight shots at the officers and four of them fell. Sergeant Bentley ran towards the man and caught hold of him by the shoulders and threw him to the ground. The man caught hold of the Sergeant's legs and pulled him down. They struggled and the man got on top of P. S. Bentley. Another man, whom I cannot describe, ran out of No. 11 and fired at Bentley, the bullet struck the man in the back and he fell backwards with his arms up in the air. I then went inside my house where I remained until the firing ceased. I heard about 15 shots fired in quick succession.

His story was plausible enough but hard to reconcile with the facts. It could not have been Bentley who caught hold of the man since he was found lying in the doorway. Possibly the boy meant Choat, but if so why did he not see Tucker and Strongman who were standing between him and the gunman. Nevertheless, the newspapers publicised him as the boy who had raised the alarm, and photographed him in youthful bowler, Eton collar, knee breeches and boots. The other inhabitants had equally sensational stories to tell. Ada Parker, at No. 2, said she was sweeping the floor when she noticed in the wooden front of the ground-floor room a small hole, about fifteen inches from the floor. Later she found a bullet at the back of the room and declared that it had passed through the bottom of her mother's long skirt and the leg of the chair she was sitting on at the time. However, Bessie Jacobs always swore that it was common knowledge the hole had been made in the chair with a red-hot poker to get money out of the reporters.

Throughout the night the police took statements and collected what evidence they could. They searched the cul-de-sac with lanterns and picked up spent ammunition-cases. Five were believed to be Mauser bullets and five Browning, and two more were unidentified. With daylight, newspaper reporters came flooding to the scene and by late morning Houndsditch was choked with sightseers.

Two more witnesses were soon found. A workman flushing gullies in Cobb Street had seen four men hurry by soon after the killings. He had heard the shots but the sound had been partly muffled by the wind and he had mistaken them for the sound of hoardings blowing down in the wind. One of the men was being supported by his friends and from his dazed expression the workman had assumed him to be drunk. Another workman made a similar statement that he had seen the same four men in Wentworth Street a little later.

The most important witness was not found until late the next afternoon. He was Isaac Levy, the manager of a tobacconist shop in Walthamstow. Immediately after the shootings he had run into Exchange Buildings and seen the policemen taken away. In the Cutlers Arms he listened afterwards to the excited babble. 'Look what a bit of luck I have had,' said Mrs Abrahams breathlessly. She had almost recovered from tripping over one of the bodies and was rapidly becoming aware of her son's importance as the only eyewitness to the killings. 'My people could have been shot down.'

Levy could no longer control himself and burst out, 'Look at mine. The men pointed revolvers at me and told me not to follow them.' Suddenly fearing that he had said too much, he hurried away and next morning caught his usual train to work. He was badly shaken by what he had read. Choat and Tucker were dead, Bentley was dying, and the condition of Bryant and Woodhams was critical. His nervousness increased. He was too afraid to go to the police but he had to tell somebody what he had seen. His later explanation for not going to the police was that he was not sure what view his firm would take of one of their managers being implicated in such an affair. He told his story again and again to his customers; one more enterprising than the rest telephoned the *Star* newspaper with the story, and they published a story in the afternoon edition that the hue and cry was for three men and a woman. By the time a *Daily Mail* reporter reached the shop, Levy had locked up, but not before telling his employers his story and asking for the rest of the afternoon off to recover his shattered nerves. His original intention had been to go home, but he steeled himself to go to Exchange Buildings, where he spoke to Chief Inspector Hayes. He was escorted by two detectives to Bishopsgate police station and after making his statement was allowed to go home, where he was run to earth by the *Daily Mail* reporter.

Levy told him that he had worked late the previous evening and his train home had pulled into Liverpool Street station at about 11.28. He followed his normal route home through Devonshire Square, Borers Passage, alongside the Port of London warehouses, and then into Cutler Street; it took him only a few minutes. As he was walking through Borers Passage he heard a single shot followed immediately by a succession of shots – fifteen or twenty he guessed – 'there was a slight interval between the first and second shots, but the others were very rapid, without any stoppage'. He ran down the passage, not very fast as he was tired, and into Cutler Street. As he turned the corner he almost bumped into the three men coming towards him. Behind them was a woman wearing a fur toque on her head and carrying a large muff. The men were in the middle of the road, only about four steps away, and he saw their faces quite clearly as there was a light burning over the carpet-maker's on the corner of the passage. The man in the centre was being supported by the other two; he seemed dazed, or exhausted, and was holding his head down. The two men on the outside both pointed revolvers into Levy's face. 'Don't follow us,' they said in broken English. 'Don't follow.' For a moment or two Levy went physically blind with fear and could see nothing. He then stood and watched them walk away down

Harrow Alley, dragging the man between them, with the woman hurrying after.

In the few minutes Constable Piper was away looking for assistance, Dubof, who had been watching him from the shadows, slipped into Exchange Buildings to tell the others that the policeman had also been to No. 12. Possibly he had made a genuine mistake and called at the wrong house, but they could not be sure. Suddenly it became impossible for them to leave. Constable Woodhams strolled into Exchange Buildings and stood in the entrance to the cul-de-sac. Now they could not get out without being stopped or seen. Still uncertain as to just how much, if anything, the police suspected, they decided to brazen it out. Max climbed back into No. 10 and resumed hammering, pausing every now and then for breath and to listen for the warning shout that would send him scrambling back over the lavatory wall. The others got ready to leave. Nina Vassilleva put on her coat and the fur toque and muff she had been given by a sick friend. The men took out their guns.

None of them had any scruples about shooting policemen. Peters had had his fingernails torn out by Tsarist police and Dubof his back torn by Cossack whips. In their own country policemen had killed, tortured and condoned the most outrageous brutalities, and there was no reason to assume that the English police were any different. Why assume they were unarmed? Fritz and Gardstein both had special pockets for concealing their guns so why shouldn't the police? Any chance of removing their fears, which were common, not only to them but to most of the East End's immigrant population at this time, was completely destroyed by their ignorance of the language.

When Bentley knocked at the door the second time Gardstein delayed opening it long enough for Nina Vassilleva, who was in the upstairs bedroom, to lean out of the back window and signal to Max to get clear. Gardstein opened the door and then went back upstairs and waited at the top of the stairs in the darkness, with only his trouser bottoms showing, as Max scrambled over the lavatory wall into the yard. Gardstein had already taken out his Mauser and was standing with it partly concealed by the folds of his overcoat when the unsuspecting Sergeant Bentley pushed open the door and stepped into the house. Less than two minutes had passed since Bentley knocked at the door. As Max scrambled clear Peters, for reasons which will be explained later, flung open the back door and walked rapidly into the room firing his Dreyse pistol. In the same instant Gardstein lifted his long-barrelled Mauser and fired at Bentley's face. His shot went through the rim of his helmet and through the shutter behind him. He saw Bentley stagger backwards, shot in the shoulder and throat by Peters. He swung his Mauser to the right and fired into Sergeant Bryant's chest as he put out his hands in front of him to ward off 'the flashes'.

Stepping over the dying Bentley sprawled in the doorway, Peters went into the street and, walking towards Sergeant Tucker wounded him with a bullet in the hip and then shot him through the heart. As Constable Strongman dragged him away Peters followed them along the street, still firing, into the light of the street lamp where Strongman had a good look at him before Peters turned back to help Gardstein.

Gardstein had been firing from the doorway as Peters cleared the street for their escape. He shot Constable Woodhams in the leg, and he was now lying unconscious in the roadway. As Nina Vassilleva scrambled downstairs and into the street Gardstein fired two more shots into the ceiling as a warning and then followed her out. Suddenly the burly figure of Constable Choat loomed out of the darkness in front of him and gripped him by the wrist. Possibly he shouted or Nina screamed for help. He pulled his Mauser trigger four times as the policeman towering over him pushed his hand down and the pistol away from his body deflecting the shots into his thigh, calf and foot. At that moment Max and Dubof ran out of the house into the street firing their guns. Peters ran behind Constable Choat and fired two closely spaced shots into his spine in the same instant that Max loosed off a shot with his Browning and hit Gardstein in the back as Constable Choat dragged him down. Max was appalled as he realised what he had done. Peters and Dubof grabbed Gardstein by the arms and, yanking him to his feet, half dragged, half carried him into Cutler Street as Constables Piper and Smoothey pounded towards them from Houndsditch. The only way they could get out now was through Borers Passage or Harrow Alley. They had almost reached Borers Passage when the tobacconist, Isaac Levy, ran out in front of them and almost collided with them head on. He had a clear view of the three men and Nina Vassileva, but did not see Max who was out of the light, somewhere in the darkness behind them, covering their retreat. Peters and Dubof lifted their pistols and pointed them at Levy's face.

Incredibly, for the next half-hour they were able to drag the badly wounded man through the East End back streets to Grove Street. Fortunately they were never stopped as they clearly had no intention of abandoning him. Nina certainly wouldn't, and after the last sighting in Harrow Alley she went with Max to a doctor who she thought might help her. The doctor flatly refused to become involved and threatened to tell the police. He then threw them out. Nina and Max could not know that he would not go to the police. From the way he reacted they genuinely thought he would. Nor could Nina have realised that Gardstein was dying otherwise she would have gone back to Grove Street. Max told her to go into hiding while he went to warn the others.

Gardstein had already borrowed a door key from Fritz to use later that night. Peters and Dubof were able to let themselves in without knocking and drag Gardstein up the dark, unlit staircase, stumbling as they did so, because there was no hand-rail to grip. They went straight to the prearranged rendezvous in the front room. As they staggered through the doorway Fritz ran over to the door and held it shut. Moments later Luba, who heard the men staggering upstairs, tried the handle. 'Don't come in,' Fritz said. She was surprised to hear his voice as she thought he was out, and went back to her room and closed the door.

Briefly, Dubof and Peters explained what had happened as

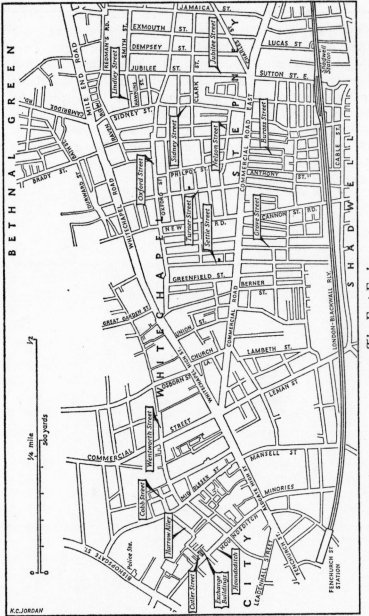

The East End

K.C.JORDAN

they bundled Gardstein onto the bed. They pulled off his shoes but left him in his overcoat as he lay there pale-faced, weak from shock and loss of blood, too ill to move. Minutes later they heard someone else come up the stairs. Either Max had borrowed the other key to let himself in or Peters and Dubof had left the door ajar. As Max came upstairs Luba opened the door of her room to see who it was; she noticed his hands, which were black with brickdust where he had been breaking through the wall. Fritz opened the door and let him in. When they heard Luba shut her door Peters and Dubof hurried downstairs without being seen, and crept into the street.

V

The Way to Dusty Death

On the morning before that of the murders, Thursday, 15 December, Fritz Svaars had woken at nine o'clock and crept out of the house at 59 Grove Street leaving his mistress still in bed. There was little point in waking her. Work had been slack and she had not gone to her brothers' shop for nearly a week. She was still asleep when he returned nearly two hours later and only woke when he touched her with his cold hands. She heard him chuckling and opened her eyes to see him standing by the bed, his cheeks red from the raw wind that was blowing outside. 'Where were you?' she said, huddling deeper into the bedclothes.

Fritz laughed. 'You'd better not ask me where I've been,' he said, and bending over her whispered, 'Get up. It's two o'clock.'

She was so much in love with him that she believed him implicitly. She got up and began to dress, but Fritz was in a playful mood and threw her clothes about the room. Luba scrambled after them and eventually lost her temper, but not for long. Fritz's good humour was infectious and they both ended up laughing. Only when she had finished dressing did Fritz show her his watch. Luba was momentarily annoyed again, remembering how deeply asleep she had been. Peter the Painter came into the room and she complained to him how Fritz had fooled her, and then pushed them both out of the room while she tidied it. Afterwards she joined them in the front room. She had not heard Gardstein come in, but when she went into the room she found him playing chess with Peter, and Fritz was in the background practising the mandoline for his part in a Christmas play at the Anarchist Club. She took some money to buy food, and Gardstein asked her to buy him some cigarettes. She jokingly replied that she would not, and when she returned and found them all drinking tea Gardstein laughingly pushed her onto the landing and told her that he would not let her in until she fetched him some cigarettes. She gave the cigarettes to Fritz and, before he and Gardstein went out together a little later, he told her to stay at home as someone was supposed to come and see him and he was to be asked to wait. After they had gone Luba made dinner and finished making a black velvet blouse for herself.

When Fritz returned at 5 p.m., Luba could see that he was not as happy as he had been in the morning. She started questioning him, but he told her curtly that he was hungry and the best thing she could do was to give him something to eat. Then, seeing that he had hurt her, he immediately put his arms around her and took her over to the food cupboard. 'Don't be angry but give me something to eat,' he said.

Fritz had spent the afternoon at 15 Duncan Terrace, Islington, in the workshop of one of the leading militant anarchists of the day, the Italian Errico Malatesta. For the past fifty years Malatesta had conspired and agitated not only in his native Italy but in England, Spain, the Levant, the United States and Argentina. On two occasions he had escaped from prison by boat – nailed up in a packing-case, if the legend is to be believed – and for the past twelve years he had lived quietly in London, running his small electrician's business, after a comrade in America had tried to shoot him. His workshop had been used for the past twelve months by a man he knew as 'the Russian'. Sometimes this unknown man used his workshop two or three times a week to finish off some little job. When he was questioned later, Malatesta always denied that he knew the man's name, or that the names he was known by – George Gardstein, Poolka Mourremitz and P. Morin – meant anything to him. He had met him at the Anarchist Club and understood that he was a Russian political refugee and engineer.

Fritz had gone down the back staircase into the workshop and introduced himself as Louis Lambert. In very bad French he asked Malatesta to sell him a cylinder of oxygen for a lantern show he was giving. Only three days before, according to Gardstein, Malatesta had exchanged a six-foot cylinder of oxygen gas for a forty-foot cylinder. When they came to cut through the safe this would give them a burning-time of about forty-five minutes. Malatesta arranged to sell him the cylinder as well as a pressure gauge, a valve and about fifteen or twenty yards of rubber tubing for which he was to pay £5. Fritz paid him £1 on account and asked for them to be ready by the following afternoon when he would send a man to collect them and pay the balance. Next day he sent a young boy, who fetched the things away on a coster's barrow. Malatesta's unknown friend, 'the Russian', was busy at the work-bench when he came. Possibly Gardstein was making sure that nothing had been missed.

Fritz's nervousness had shown itself in a more marked form the previous Saturday when he had gone to the British Asbestos Company, Commercial Road, to buy the asbestos boards they needed to guard against the heat when they were cutting open the back of the safe. His English was even more limited than his French. When he could not make himself understood he began shouting at the woman who was trying to serve him. He made so much noise that the Company Secretary came out of his office and personally intervened. He called the warehouseman and told him to show Fritz some asbestos boards but none of them, it seemed, were thick enough, and Fritz had only the vaguest notion of what he wanted. Eventually he chose four boards but refused to pay the price (17s 3d), saying it was too much. The Company Secretary again had to intervene; he told Fritz that he had better make up his mind as they were closing in a few minutes and, more bluntly, that he was going to a football match and would not serve him. In the end, Fritz picked two cheaper boards, paid 8s 6d and left.

He was obviously in the same tense mood when he came back from Malatesta's. Luba ignored him but after they had eaten he and Peter, who ate with them, started talking in Lettish. She railed at them for talking in a language which they knew she did not understand. Peter went back to his own room and left her with Fritz, who quietly washed up, put the things away and then sat down on the bed beside her, talking about the concert he had arranged for the Russian emigrants. She heard him rehearse his lines for the Russian socialist play he was appearing in on Boxing Night. He had reluctantly agreed to take the part of a policeman hunting down socialist revolutionaries because nobody else would. He translated his lines from the Lettish into Russian for her so that she could understand. The original play, *Matteo Falcone*, was the story of a Corsican brigand whose son betrayed one of his comrades to the soldiers. To wipe out the dishonour Matteo Falcone must kill his son Fortunato, and makes him stand on a small mount while he prepares to shoot him. From the mount Fortunato sees the captured brigand escape from the soldiers and run back towards him. Fortunato wipes out his dishonour by fighting the soldiers and defending the brigand he has so recently betrayed. In the version in which Fritz was playing, the soldiers became policemen and Fritz was the inspector leading them. There was one important change in the text. The boy who betrayed the brigand/social revolutionary could not wipe out the dishonour. He was shot.

They sat on the bed until it grew dark. Luba listened to him as he softly repeated his lines in Russian; she might not have been so happy had she known that the boy's part was being played by a Russian girl and that Fritz had told her that he was unattached. She nestled closer. Suddenly somebody outside the room shouted, 'What are you doing in there?' and broke the mood. The door was pushed open and Joseph and Gardstein came into the room. One of them struck a match and said, 'We shall not disturb them.' As Luba swung her legs off the bed to light the gas her face filled with disgust as she saw Joseph bend over Fritz and whisper in his ear. Fritz spoke low and then,

seeing the look on Luba's face, told her to go into the other room
as Joseph had something to show him which it would not be
nice for her to see. He followed her to the door and told her that
he would explain later. She went sullenly into the other room
where Peter sat reading. She stayed with him for a bit and then
went out. She returned just before midnight. Fritz looked at her
coldly and asked where she'd been. Luba smiled wanly. 'Fat lot
you care about me,' she said. She waited for him to say something else but he ignored her and continued to leaf through
the papers he had taken from the drawer he normally kept
locked. He put some on the fire and watched them burn.
'Papers lie about here for a hundred years,' he said. And then
with a change of emphasis. 'They ought to be burned.'

'Whose fault is it?' Luba snapped, and walked out onto the
landing and into Peter's room. Her head drooped, she wrote, as
if the whole world had come to an end. Peter looked at her
thoughtfully for several minutes and then went into the other
room to speak to Fritz.

She stayed in bed the next morning, the day of the murders, until 12.30 p.m., and then went to her brother's shop to ask
him to cut out a dress for her. In the street she passed Gardstein
and Hoffman. She deliberately ignored them but guessed they
were on their way to see Fritz. Possessiveness, as much as curiosity, made her hurry back to find out what they were doing.
From the murmur in the front bedroom it was obvious that
there were a number of visitors. She went in and asked Fritz
for some money to buy food; she then complained that she was
not feeling well and asked her friend, Sara Trassjonsky, who
was in the back room waiting for her, if she would go to the
shop instead. Sara was a Polish Jewess who had been working
for Luba's brother since her arrival from Paris a few months
before. She was showing increasing signs of mental instability.
Part of her condition was certainly physical. Her right shoulder-
blade was deformed, as was her left hip. She was a willing little
creature and went to the shop readily enough. She had only
been gone a few minutes when Luba, on the pretext that she
wanted some rubber heels, went once more into the room to call

to her from the window; but Sara was too far down the street to hear. Maddeningly she next insisted on taking down the curtains as she wanted to send them to the laundry. The men had ignored her previous remarks that she was not feeling well, but now one or two faces were tinged with amusement and several pitying glances were thrown at Fritz, who went on talking animatedly to Gardstein.

The talk became even more restrained when an unexpected visitor dropped in, a young balalaika-player who had been teaching Fritz for the past three weeks to play the mandoline for his part in the Boxing Night play. He was a thin-faced twenty-one year-old named Nicholas Tomacoff, with dark hair and a small moustache, who had arrived in England in June from St Petersburg where he had been living with three maiden aunts who owned a tailor's business. Tomacoff played regularly with a local group of Russian balalaika-players and singers, the Slavonics, who were well known in the area. In November Fritz had called at his lodgings and asked if he would play the mandoline one evening at the club in Jubilee Street. Tomacoff had agreed, although his only payment would be lemonade, and on the night of the performance Fritz had worked the stage curtains. They had spent the rest of the evening talking, and a casual friendship sprung up between them. Sometimes they used to meet four and five times a week. It was several weeks before Fritz trusted him enough to give him his address, but after that they visited each other's lodgings very frequently. Tomacoff learned that Fritz carried a Browning revolver, that he also possessed a Mauser which he had bought in Antwerp (there was a broken one lying openly on a shelf) and that there were several hundred rounds of ammunition in the room.

Tomacoff knew some of the other men slightly; he had met Gardstein, Dubof and Hoffman several times. John Rosen was pointed out to him as 'the Barber'; he had stripped off his coat and waistcoat and was playing chess with 'the Painter'. Joseph was sitting on the bed and Osip Federoff lying down. He stayed till about 2 p.m., walking about the room, strumming his mandoline and listening to the conversation.

The others stayed talking till about five, finalising the arrangements for the robbery; they drifted off in ones and twos, and when most of them had gone Fritz told Luba that he was going up to the West End to collect some money that was owing to him. She argued with him, but he told her that he could only get the money by going there personally. He said that he might stop the night but would be back by eleven next morning. Seeing that he was determined to go, Luba pretended indifference and asked for some money to go to the pictures. She watched him leave the house with Joseph, and only Peter Piaktow was left behind when she went out at 5.30 p.m.

Sara joined her and they returned at about 9.30 p.m. In their absence Fritz and Joseph came back and waited in the front bedroom with Peter. When the women came in Peter played his violin. As expected, Luba stayed away; their relationship could not have been worse. Luba's dislike of him stemmed from the fact that preferential treatment was given to Peter. It was typical that, after the quarrel between Luba and Fritz the previous evening, Peter had simply got up and walked out. And when she and Sara returned home from the pictures there was no friendly greeting, no suggestion that he should join them for a bedtime drink, no friendly word shouted through the closed door as might happen in a normal relationship. From the gang's point of view it was an ideal situation.

Sara left the house briefly but soon returned; she was staying the night. After supper she and Luba sat in bed reading. At about 12.30 a.m. they heard two or three people struggling up the stairs in the dark. There was no hand-rail and one false move could easily tip them into the staircase well. The women were terrified and listened as the footsteps reached the front bedroom where Peter was. Luba slipped onto the landing and nervously tried to open the front-bedroom door. Someone was leaning against it and to her astonishment she heard Fritz's voice. 'Don't come in,' he called out. She went back to her room and closed the door but opened it again a moment later when she heard someone else on the stairs. It was Max. His hands, she noticed, were black and he was in a highly excitable state. He too went into the front bedroom. Soon afterwards – it was only minutes at the most – she and Sara heard two people going downstairs. Then silence.

Suddenly Fritz opened the door. Ignoring Luba he said to Sara: 'Mourremitz is shot; make him a cold compress.' Only then did Fritz turn to Luba and ask her for one of the two sovereigns he had given her to buy a dress with earlier in the week. She begged him to tell her what had happened, but he ignored her questions and told her that she had better get out of the house. He stayed only five minutes and then left with Max, Peter and Joseph, who had been watching silently in the background.

Gardstein was fully conscious and lying on the bed. His overcoat had been flung to one side, and Sara pulled off his boots. She lifted his shirt and gently placed a wet towel in position on his back. Luba shuddered and said that she could do nothing for him as she was feeling too ill. The gang meant nothing to her and not even out of pity would she stay. It was obviously best to get her out of the way altogether. Sara gave her the key to her own rooms in 10 Settle Street.

Instead Luba went to 36 Lindley Street where Karl Hoffman lived; she and Fritz had frequently fed him when he had no money. He rented one room on the first floor; he was so poor that the rent had been reduced from 3s 6d to 3s a week. On the ground floor was Morris Reitman, his wife and three children. Mrs Reitman, or Mrs Morris as she was generally known, was so fat that she was known as 'Grobber' Morris. Her size had become even more startling in the last nine months and when Luba knocked at the door she was just starting a difficult labour. The midwife was with her in the back room, and Morris Reitman was sitting in darkness in the front room with his three children when he heard Luba knock at the door. He listened for the number of knocks. Twice was always for Hoffman upstairs, although he did not know his name. Curious to see who was knocking at this hour, he peeped into the badly lit passage. He saw that the woman was not wearing a hat and that her coat and hair were dark.

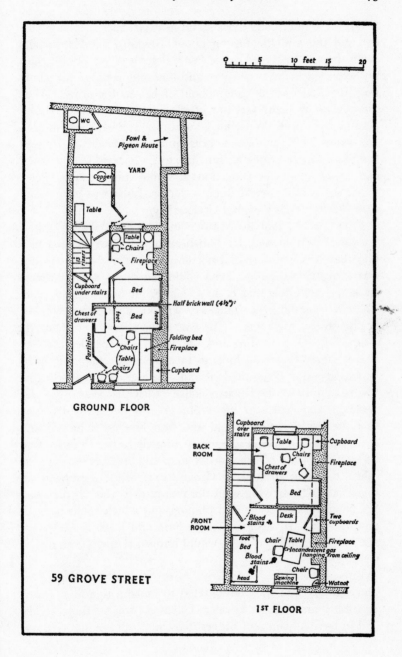

GROUND FLOOR

59 GROVE STREET

1ST FLOOR

On the way upstairs Luba could hear Grobber Morris groaning and the midwife fussing about. Stepping into Hoffman's room she was staggered to see Fritz, Peter and Joseph. She had not expected them to be there and had only come to ask Hoffman for advice. Fritz caught hold of her by the arms. 'What are you doing here? Get out of it at once,' he shouted. Luba became hysterical. 'What have you brought a wounded man to our rooms for?' she sobbed. Fritz quietened her down. He told her to go to her brothers', but first to go back to Grove Street and bring away her collection of family photographs. Peter Piaktow, he said, would fetch a doctor. Luba was not to stay with Gardstein. He gave her his door key.

Fritz checked that his Mauser and the Browning Max had borrowed were loaded. He had been appalled when Max told him that Nina's doctor had not only refused to help them but was going to the police. Fritz could not prove his innocence. Luba did not know that he had been in the house all the time. There was nothing he could say without implicating himself, or the others, still more. If he was caught, even supposing he escaped hanging in England, he could still be deported to Russia where he would have to face a capital charge. Besides, he was afraid of being made to talk. He had confessed when he was beaten up by the Russian police earlier that year – this was common knowledge in the group – and he firmly believed that the British police would also beat him up if he fell into their hands. He was ready to kill himself rather than let that happen. In view of what Max had said, neither he nor the others dared to go back to Grove Street, if, as they believed, the doctor was arriving with the police, even though they had left behind them letters and photographs which could incriminate them all. It was safer to use Sara and Luba as they were not involved, and very little would happen to them even if they were caught.

Luba hurried back to Grove Street and snatched up some photographs. She was too agitated to make a thorough search and told Sara to leave at once. Gardstein was writhing on the bed in terrible pain and begged Sara not to leave him. He was so ill that she felt she could not abandon him and told him that she would stay. But Luba scuttled away to Sara's lodgings. At 3 a.m. Gardstein's condition worsened still more, but the pain was more manageable and he told Sara to leave him as he knew he was dying. Instead she went to her lodgings and insisted that Luba help her to find a doctor. Luba thought she knew where there was one in the Whitechapel Road. She did not know the number, but there was a brass plate outside in both Yiddish and English.

They pulled their shawls over their heads and hurried through the dark, deserted streets until they found the doctor's house just before 3.30 a.m. There was a speaking tube from the street to the upstairs bedroom where the duty doctor, John Scanlon, was sleeping. Although the brass plate was inscribed in both Yiddish and English, Dr Scanlon could only speak English, which neither woman knew. Fortunately he could speak French and Sara, who had lived in France for some time, told him, 'A man is very bad at 59 Grove Street.' She gave no further explanation. As Scanlon came out Luba pulled her shawl further over her face so that she would not be recognised. After she had walked along with them for just a few minutes, she slipped quietly away and went back to Sara's lodgings.

It was not until they got to 59 Grove Street that Sara realised she had taken with her the door key. Reluctantly she knocked on the door to wake the landlord. She tried several times to attract his attention. Dr Scanlon became tired of waiting and rapped imperiously on the wooden shutters with his stick. At last the door opened. As Dr Scanlon climbed the stairs, keeping well over to one side away from the missing hand-rail, he heard the door slam behind them in protest.

He noticed that the front-bedroom door was slightly ajar. The gas light was faint and had almost gone out. The walls were covered with a gaudy paper and two or three cheap theatrical prints, and the bare boards littered with cigarette butts and spent matches. Facing the door was a narrow iron bedstead painted green. On the bed and on the floor were scattered blood-stained towels, and the bed-linen and the pillow where the man was lying were also spattered with blood.

Gardstein was dressed except for his boots and when he saw the doctor he muttered to himself. He explained that he had been shot, accidentally, in the back three hours previously by a friend. From his examination Dr Scanlon concluded that there was evidence of a bullet lodged in the front of the chest. Later, it was found to be touching the right ventricle. He suggested that Gardstein should be taken immediately to the London Hospital, but this was flatly rejected by the dying man. In the circumstances there was little else the doctor could do except to promise to call later and to give him some medicine, which Sara could go and collect with him now, to deaden the pain. He asked what name he should put on the medical certificate and was told George Gardstein. He then said that his fee was ten shillings. Gardstein told Sara to look in his pockets. She found a sovereign and put the change by the bed.

Sara went back with Dr Scanlon to his surgery for the medicine and then went on to 36 Lindley Street where the men were still hiding. She told Fritz that Gardstein knew he was dying and was worried because the papers had not been burnt. Fritz told her to bring him some clothes, any photographs she could find and the ship's tickets for Australia (see above, page 48). If Gardstein died, she was to pour petrol on his body and on his bed and burn the house down to destroy all evidence.

Sara again went to 59 Grove Street. She gave Gardstein some medicine and nursed him until 7 a.m., when he again told her to leave him as she could do him no good. She went to her lodgings and lay down, still in her clothes, on the bed; she was exhausted. After she had rested for a while she went back to the dying man. She offered him some more medicine, but he refused to take it. He again told her to go away as there was nothing more she could do.

By this time, Sara was close to breaking-point. Neither she nor Luba knew what to do next. They told Mr Reuben, the grocer in Old Montagu Street, about Gardstein, but Mrs Reuben came to the door and told them to go away as she and her husband did not want to be involved. Sara felt that she had to go to the dying Gardstein once more, and this time Luba, who had at last stifled her fear, went with her. It was now 9.15 a.m. Luba, out of habit, knocked on the door, and it was opened by her landlord Max Katz. He was still standing by the open door, fastening his collar, when the two women ran back downstairs with terrified looks on their faces. As they hurried into the street he went upstairs and peered into the front bedroom. Lying on the bed, which was littered with blood-stained sheets and towels, was Gardstein's dead body.

Luba was too terrified to go home. She borrowed some clothes from a friend and went to 36 Lindley Street. But Fritz, Joseph and Peter had already gone; only Hoffman was there. She asked the same questions over and over again. Where was Fritz? What had happened? Hoffman would tell her nothing. While they were talking a friend of Peter's, Pavell Molchanoff, who had known him in Marseilles in 1909, came in. Luba at once told him all she knew and begged him to go to the house and collect the photographs she had left behind. She was terrified, she said, of being accused of Gardstein's murder. She pleaded with Sara to return with him to the house while she waited for them both in Pavell's lodgings in 36 Havering Street. When she got there she was not sure which room to go into. She hesitated for a moment and then went into the front room. As she entered the young balalaika-player, Nicholas Tomacoff, got up and shook her hand. The other men there were having an animated conversation and, not wanting to be the only woman present, she went into the back room to wait; opening the door she stared with astonishment into the clean-shaven face of Peter the Painter.

Pavell Molchanoff had known that she would find him there but hadn't said anything. Peter had banged on his door at 2 a.m. asking to be put up for the night as it was too late for him to get into his own lodgings. When Luba told him that Gardstein was dead he became very agitated and paced restlessly up and down the room. He ignored her questions and said that he could not tell her anything of what had happened.

As she became more frightened she asked if she should leave the country. Peter asked her if she had any money. As she was looking into her purse Pavell came into the room alone. His news was bad. When he and Sara had tried to leave the landlord had told him that one or other of them must remain. Quite what he intended to do they did not know – it is doubtful whether he knew himself – but Sara had had to stay as hostage.

Peter hurriedly put on his coat and waistcoat and asked how much it would cost to get to Poplar. Pavell gave Luba the half-sovereign, change from Dr Scanlon's fee, which he had taken from the bedside table. Peter asked her for some of it, and she gave him half a crown. Luba said that she would go to her brothers' house and wait until Pavell and Hoffman called later in the day, as they had promised. When she reached home she heard her two younger brothers talking excitedly about the Houndsditch murders. Luba felt instinctively that they were connected in some way with Gardstein's death.

Meanwhile, Sara was waiting beside Gardstein's body for something to happen. Already her delicate mental balance threatened to topple over into insanity. While she waited she picked up papers and photographs and burnt them in the grate but there were periods of blackness and depression, which gradually grew longer as the morning progressed, when she would sit in front of the small jets of flame and stare blankly into nothingness.

Clearly the landlord had no intention of doing anything except keep her there and wait on events; but Dr Scanlon had a clear duty to inform the police. He had been called to attend a dying man suffering with a bullet wound which he knew could not possibly have been self-inflicted, and the circumstances were such that he must have strongly suspected foul play. But there were strong reasons of self-preservation for not going to the police. Most immigrants, particularly those from Russia and the countries under its domination, believed that there was little or no difference between the Tsarist police system, which used murder and torture and systematically carried out pogroms against a suffering population, and the English policeman.

Already, by late Saturday morning, there was astonishment among the Russian immigrants that the police had not carried out a pogrom. If Scanlon had told the police what he had seen and this information had got back, he would instantly have been branded as a police informer by every immigrant and his practice shunned. He therefore delayed telephoning the local police at Arbour Square until just before it was time to make his midday visit.

His information was passed on to Detective Inspector Frederick Porter Wensley, nicknamed 'the Weasel' and, by foreigners who could not pronounce the word, 'Vensel', an animal he in no way physically resembled. In fact, his small dark eyes, the long nose, the brushed-back hair and the face sloping downwards from the narrow skull to the broad heavy jaw and jowls made him resemble more accurately a sorrowful elephant, an unfortunate impression which the luxuriant walrus-moustache did something to eradicate. He was a Somerset man who had joined the Metropolitan Police in 1887. Part of his probation had been spent in Whitechapel during the Jack the Ripper murders, and two years after he joined he was transferred to H Division permanently. At first he was resentful of the transfer but gradually he adjusted to Whitechapel and came to enjoy it. His overriding ambition was to become a detective but he was too keen for some of his colleagues, and in spite of his dogged devotion to duty he was held back until the divisional superintendent insisted that he should be taken into the department. Again he was denied promotion, and after four years he asked for an explanation. He was told that promotion would mean his automatic transfer to another division and he had become too useful to the department. He immediately appealed to the Assistant Commissioner to intervene. A special exception was made in his case and, instead of automatic transfer to another division each time he was promoted, he was kept where he was.

Wensley contacted the City Police and he was soon joined by Detective Inspector Thompson. Because of Wensley's own unrivalled knowledge of the East End it was arranged for him to collaborate in the investigation. The two men hurried to Dr Scanlon's surgery and told the doctor to make his call on Gardstein and then return to his surgery where they would be waiting for him. In this way he would not be connected with the raid that would inevitably follow. The doctor stressed again – he was most insistent on the point – that nothing should be said or done to indicate to anyone that he had helped them. The detectives agreed; they only asked one thing of him in return; it was vital that he should tell no one, and most particularly the Press, what was happening.

The doctor's visit to 59 Grove Street is unrecorded, but he must have seen the brooding figure of Sara Trassjonsky as well as the stiffening corpse. He got past the landlord and then, ignoring everything he had been told, telephoned the Coroner's Officer; it was either the Coroner's Officer or Dr Scanlon himself who then gave the story to the press. When he got back to the surgery he told the astounded policemen what he had done. They were furious and raced with several armed detectives to the house, reaching it only minutes before the reporters.

Mrs Katz – 'a fat old Jewess' was Wensley's unflattering description – opened the door. She could not or would not understand their questions, not even when Wensley cut short her babble and pushed her up the stairs ahead of him, guessing that if there were armed men at the head of the stairs no power on earth would have got her up. (He reckoned that her ample bulk would protect him from any possible bullet, but her weight would have crushed him if she had fallen backwards!)

As the bedroom door swung open, he saw Gardstein lying on the bed with his eyes open, facing them. It was hard to believe that he was dead. He was lying there in a crumpled dark-grey suit and white shirt, with white stripe facings, pulled out at the waistband.

Detective Sergeant Benjamin Leeson, who had joined Wensley, pushed open the door of the back room. Sara Trassjonsky was thrusting more papers into the flames as he reached forward, his revolver ready, and seized the hunchbacked little woman by the wrist. She was hustled away to City Police headquarters in Old Jewry, off Cheapside, and policemen were stationed outside the house to keep out the reporters milling about on the pavement. A young man pushed through the small crowd and, ignoring the policeman outside, knocked on the door. When it was opened he asked for Fritz. His name, he told the astonished detectives, was Nicholas Tomacoff.

VI

A Face like Adonis

A *Daily Chronicle* reporter who visited the house in Grove Street wrote:

The street door opens into a narrow and ill-lighted passage, in which badly washed and ragged clothing was hanging from bits of string. Towards the end of the passage a sharp turn to the left led me on to a narrow and almost perpendicular staircase, without handrail. Here was more washing suspended from the ceiling. At the top of a staircase was a small landing, and immediately in front was the room in which the assassin died.

The room itself is about ten feet by nine, and about seven feet high. A gaudy paper decorates the walls and two or three cheap theatrical prints are pinned up. A narrow iron bedstead painted green, with a peculiarly shaped head and foot faces the door. On the bedstead was a torn and dirty woollen mattress, a quantity of blood-stained clothing, a blood-stained pillow and several towels also saturated with blood.

Under the window stood a string sewing machine, and a rickety table, covered with a piece of mole cloth, occupied the centre of the room. On it stood a cup and plate, a broken glass, a knife and fork, and a couple of bottles and a medicine bottle. Strangely contrasting with the dirt and squalor, a painted wooden sword lay on the table, and another, to which was attached a belt of silver paper, lay on a broken desk supported on a stool. On the mantelpiece and on a cheap whatnot stood tawdry ornaments. In an open cupboard beside the fireplace were a few more pieces of crockery, a tin or two, and a small piece of bread. A mean and torn blind and a strip of curtain protected the window, and a roll of surgeon's lint on the desk. The floor was bare and dirty, and, like the fireplace, littered with burnt matches and cigarette ends – altogether a dismal and wretched place to which the wounded desperado had been carried to die.

On the bedside table was a tweed cap containing a handful of ammunition – six ·297/·230 short cartridges for Morris-tube and small rook rifles, six .30 Mauser pistol-cartridges and seventeen 7.9 mm Mauser rifle-cartridges of Austrian 1904 manufacture – gathered together and put there by Sara Trass-jonsky as she ransacked the room. In Gardstein's jacket and trousers pockets were thirty 7.65 mm Belgian cartridges of F. N. manufacture and in the dark overcoat, with a bullet hole in the back, that was slipped over the end of the bed a clip of seven cartridges and seven more loose of the same make. Thrust between the mattress and the palliasse was a loaded Dreyse pistol and two more clips of ammunition.

Two immediate links with the shootings were two uphol-stered chairs matching four others in 11 Exchange Buildings, and the door key of No. 9 which was found in Gardstein's pocket.

The papers which were found scattered about the room and in Sara's lodgings, which had been taken there by her and Luba in the night, firmly dispelled police doubts that they were deal-ing with the usual criminal gang. In Gardstein's pocket book was a member's card, dated 2 July 1910, certifying that the bearer was a member of the Lettish Anarchist Communist Group 'Leesma', as well as detailed instructions for exploding bombs by electricity, exploding quicksilver, stuff for fuses, and the specifications of several guns including their calibre, length and weight. There were also two letters from Zürich, one apparently from his brother complaining that he had worked all summer like a mad dog but could not save a farthing and hoping that Gardstein, at least, would have had a full purse. There was one cryptic line, 'Have you written to the finger of God in Libau?' He ended, 'The devil take it, I have spent 15 francs although I have not much money.' The other letter was also from Zürich asking him to send some money to buy an overcoat. Gardstein was also carrying a passport in the name of Schafshi Khan.

The core of Fritz's letters that survived referred to prisoners in the Central Prison, Riga, and were nearly all addressed from the Hard Labour Section. His main correspondent was Charles who, in one letter, complained of the number of 'dogs' (spies) that were already hovering around. One friend is sentenced to two years' imprisonment and another is sent to Siberia. In his longest letter to survive Charles complained of the anguish of seeing their friends suffer and how helpless he was to help them. Mary (he mentions her Christian name only) was sentenced to ten years' imprisonment less $3\frac{1}{2}$ months she was awaiting trial. Bail was fixed at 1000 roubles (£100), but it was impossible to raise such a sum. Now she was in N–4.

All around I see awful things which I cannot tell you. I do not blame our friends as they are doing all that is possible, but things are not getting better.

The life of the workman is full of pain and suffering, but if the suffering reaches a certain degree one wonders whether it would not be better to follow the example of Rainis [an author of Lettish poems] who says burn at once so that you may not suffer long, but one feels that one cannot do it although it seems very advisable. The outlook is always the same, awful outlook for which we must sacrifice our strength. There is not and cannot be another outlet. Under such circumstances, our better feelings are at war with those who live upon our labour. The weakest part of our organisation is that we cannot do sufficient for our friends who are falling. For instance, such an incident occurred last week. I had to send 10 roubles to Milau Prison for S. Cerman who is to be transferred to another prison. I [also] had to secure the necessary for Krustmadi, and this evening I received news from Libau prison that one of our friends of last summer has been taken there without any money. We ought to help but we have only 33 kopecks and the treasury of the Red X is quite empty. It is terrible because the prisoner may think we will not help him!

A more personal demand was from Fritz's sister Liza, who was two years older. In September she wrote to him from Hamburg advising him against carrying on with a Jewish girl as he already had a wife. Between June and September she had been ill in hospital, it was thought with tuberculosis, and the money she had saved from teaching had been spent, as well as their parents' money, on doctors' bills. She still hoped to join him one day, but on the next realised that she never would. Some of the cards and letters the police found were unintelligible without the code. Written on one postcard was 'They who live in Neva Street have received, as you ask me to get the information'; another began with the verse of 'A Dog' (A Spy?), and two more were about an old miller woman who grumbled that she had been forgotten. There were personal cards and letters belonging to Peter the Painter from his girlfriend, Anna Schwarz living in Kiev – they were mostly love messages. 'The Moon is for the night/The Sun is for the day/But your eyes are always for me!' 'This is my picture. I have had two more taken. This is your old wife. If you have no money I will send your money back.' She always referred to herself as 'your black girl'. There were others asking whether he is going to give her up, should she wear her hair long or short, and how did he like her in this Russian costume?

Other letters were from an unknown correspondent in Baku, where there was a Lettish Society of about 200 members. There was correspondence with the Lettish group Zensonis ('Industrious'), Brihwiba and the Black Flag, the largest group in Paris; a statement of accounts from the Executive Committee of the Social Revolutionary Party in Baku with the motto 'In the fight you will get your right'; a collection list for impartial prisoners belonging to no party to make their suffering easier; notices to prisoners in Riga and leaflets against conscription. Running through the whole of the correspondence which survived – and one can safely assume that the furrow was just as deeply ploughed in the correspondence Sara burnt – is a constant plea for money.

Before the body was taken away, or Sara Trassjonsky to the

station, Inspector Thompson brought the boy Solomon Abrahams from Exchange Buildings – he was as far as they knew at that time the only witness to the shootings – to the house to make a positive identification. Whether by chance or by design – one suspects the latter – he saw Sara Trassjonsky as she was being taken away and identified her as one of the people he had seen. He said he recognised her because of her hunchback. The body was then taken away and, after the post mortem, photographed and placed in a special apparatus for preserving it. A journalist was dining at the London Hospital when a young medical student came in and said excitedly, 'We've got him. There was great competition, and he's as handsome as Adonis – a very beautiful corpse.'

By Sunday evening, 18 December, several more pieces had fallen into place. Most important was the willingness of Tomacoff to help the police. Within hours he had given them a complete list and description of the men he had seen the previous afternoon in Fritz's room, together with the names of those he knew. He also knew the address of the locksmith, Osip Federoff, who had carelessly given it to him. On the Sunday evening, between seven and eight o'clock, Tomacoff took the police to Federoff's lodgings at 141 Romford Street. He was lying on his bed when Tomacoff knocked on the door of his room and told him to get up as the police were outside waiting. He also took them to 36 Havering Street where Peter Piaktow and Pavell Molehanoff, who had accompanied Sara Trassjonsky to Grove Street, had spent the night.

When Luba had left Pavell at Saturday lunchtime and gone to her mother's home, Pavell had promised to call and see her later that day. At 5 p.m. he had arrived with a newspaper containing a description of the woman who was wanted in connection with the murders. Its very vagueness made Luba suspect that it was her, though in fact it was a description of Nina Vassilleva. It was also the first time that she had heard a full account of what had happened. She was naturally terrified. She did not dare to tell her mother or her elder brothers, and asked

Pavell if he could find her a room where she could hide. Pavell said that he would try but his efforts proved unsuccessful. Luba then asked a girl, Esther Weiner, lodging with her mother, if she would go to Sara Trassjonsky's lodgings and pick up some photographs. Esther agreed. Presumably Luba told her something of what had happened, because the girl took her to her sister's house at 41 Great Garden Street while she went alone to Sara's lodgings. On arrival at 10 Settle Street Esther was arrested by the waiting policemen and not released until late the next morning. Then she told Luba's mother what had happened and her brothers, Jack and Nathan, went looking for Luba.

When Esther did not return, Luba left at 11 p.m. and went to a friend in Columbia Road. She begged to be allowed to stay but was told there wasn't the room. One of the lodgers took her to a house somewhere near Victoria Park Road and she spent the night there. In the morning, about eight, the landlord burst into her room and told her to get out as her description was in the morning papers. Wearily she dragged herself back to Columbia Road where her brothers found her. They dragged her to Leman Street police station. Sergeant Mackenzie was at the desk when they brought her in. 'This is the young woman the police are looking for,' they said fiercely. 'She lived at 59 Grove Street, in the back room first floor, where the dead man was found yesterday, with a man named Fritz.'

The printed description of the woman wanted for questioning was 'Age 26 to 30; 5ft 4 in; slim build, full breasts; complexion medium, face drawn; eyes blue; hair brown; dress, dark blue, three quarters jacket and skirt, white blouse, large black hat trimmed with silk'. But it was such a vague description that nobody, least of all Isaac and Fanny Gordon, connected it with their own lodger, Nina Vassilleva. As far as they knew she was still living in the country where, after three weeks nursing a sick friend, she had gone to manage a small cigarette-making business for her employer, who was also ill. She had already been gone a further three weeks. About 8 p.m., nearly twenty-four hours after the murders, Isaac went into her room to put a penny in the meter as the gas was fading. He realised with a shock that somebody was lying on the bed. In the darkness he could only see the body outline. He was relieved at hearing the familiar tones of Nina Vassilleva, but when he turned up the gas he was appalled by the change in her appearance. Her hair had been dyed a harsh, ugly black and she was clearly showing tremendous signs of strain. He called to his wife, who had gone to the yard to fetch some water, and she gently persuaded Nina to get up.

Nina followed them into the front parlour with ill-concealed reluctance and after only a few minutes' stay went back to her own room. Fanny Gordon tried to question her but Nina only wanted to know what had been happening in London. 'There is no good news in London,' Fanny said, and added almost as an afterthought, 'but there has been a pogrom yesterday and some of the police have been shot and murdered.' Later, when she had gone and her twelve-year-old daughter Polly came into the room to pick up the school books she kept on the dresser, Nina asked her to fetch a newspaper and read to her what it said about the Houndsditch murders. She sat on the bed and listened intently as the child read every scrap of news about the murders, including the description of the woman wanted for questioning. Afterwards she saw Nina measuring herself to see how tall she was.

Isaac Gordon waited until his wife and daughter had gone to bed and then he went into Nina's room. She was kneeling in front of the grate burning a mass of letters and papers and in a completely hysterical state. He begged her not to burn the papers. 'This is not right of you to burn [them] like this, it is not right.' Hysterically she told him that she was the woman who had been living in Exchange Buildings and that she had heard that the police were going to carry out house-to-house searches; she did not want them to find these papers. Isaac pleaded with her to let him have them for safe keeping. 'You must not burn any papers as I can take them [to a place] where they will be looked after. You can trust me as I have known you for eight

months. Your friends come here and I do not talk to anyone,'
he wheedled. He went to bed but spent a restless night, as he
thought that in such an overwrought state Nina might kill herself. At 8 a.m. he knocked again on her door and it was only
when he knocked for a third time that she let him in. She
climbed back into bed and said that she felt ill. 'Don't make
life any more miserable,' Isaac implored.

'It would have been better if they had shot me,' Nina
answered, 'instead of the man they have shot. He was the best
friend I had.'

'You need not go on like that because he is dead and you
can't fetch him back,' Isaac told her brutally.

'Without him I might just as well be dead,' she cried. Lifting
her head from the pillow she took a brown-paper parcel and
handed it to Isaac for safe keeping.

For the rest of the day she brooded and in the evening got
up to wash her hair with spirit vinegar soda to take out the dye.
She was disturbed by a knock on the door. When she opened it
John Rosen was standing there. 'Have you brought trouble,'
she asked coldly. He gave a slight shrug. 'I don't know.' She
did not care to talk but told him that she had left the house
when the men went in to commit the robbery. Rosen watched
her brush her naturally brown hair which was streaked with
large patches of black dye, and then left after ten to fifteen
minutes' hesitant conversation. He had only been gone ten
minutes when there was a second knock on the door and
Detective Inspector Wensley walked in.

The instigator of this visit was Isaac Gordon, who had taken
the parcel for safe keeping to his son-in-law, who had quickly
wheedled the secret out of him. He had then persuaded him to
take the parcel to Arbour Square police station and had gone
along to interpret for him. A cursory examination showed that
it contained a passport issued to Minna, daughter of Indrik
Gristis, a peasant woman resident in Courland, some papers,
photographs and several books including *History of the Revolutionary Movement in Russia, On the Revolution and on
Revolutionary Government, A Tale about an Unrighteous Czar,*

The Government: Its Role in History and Positive Science. The photographs were now in Wensley's pocket. He ignored the dyed hair and kept his questions to a minimum. Nina, it seemed, did know a little English and could answer him if he spoke slowly. Her name, she said, was Lena Vasilev. ('I am a Russian, I make cigarettes.') Wensley asked if she was a member of the Anarchist Club. She denied this but admitted having gone there on several occasions.

'Do you know that some police officers were shot at Houndsditch on Friday night?'

'I heard of it.'

'Some of the men who were engaged in the shooting are said to have been members of the Club. Do you know them?'

'Perhaps I do, perhaps I don't.'

'We are told you have been from home three weeks and you only came back yesterday?'

'That's a lie. I have always been here.'

'I am also told you have some bullets and cartridges here.' This was a complete fabrication but Wensley was looking for an opening and she handed it to him.

'I haven't but you can look, gentlemen, if you like.'

Wensley had no doubt that they had found the woman they wanted. Among her clothes was a dark-blue jacket and skirt fitting the description, and on the front of her coat were large stains of what appeared to be blood. She also fitted the witnesses' descriptions perfectly. Wensley decided not to arrest her, in the hope that she would lead them to the rest of the gang. As yet she did not know of Isaac Gordon's betrayal; she was stunned when Wensley reached into his pocket and laid in front of her the photographs she had placed in the brown-paper parcel. One of them was of Gardstein. As she stared at them Wensley asked, 'Whose photos are these?' In his pocket was the last one – the thirteenth – of Nina herself.

'I don't know,' she answered.

She could not understand why he let her go. Next morning she said she felt ill and asked Isaac Gordon to go to a doctor

1 The Tottenham Outrage

(a) The capture of the tram
(*Radio Times Hulton Picture Library*)

(b) The bedroom in Oak Cottage where Jacob shot himself

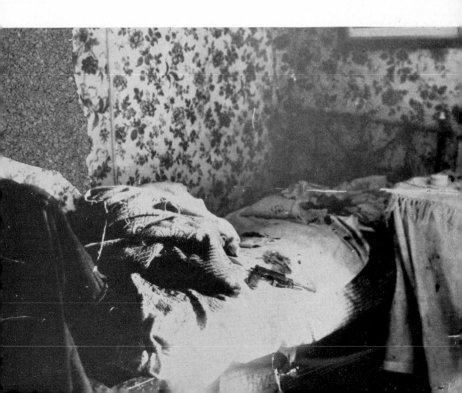

2 *(a)* Karl Hoffman, Jacob Fogel, 'Bifsteks'

(b) George Gardstein

(c) Karl Hoffman at the time of his arrest

(d) Max Smoller

3 *(a)* Jacob Peters at the time of
his arrest

(b) Yourka Dubof

(c) Nina Vassilleva

(d) John Rosen

THE DAILY GRAPHIC

ONE PENNY

LONDON: MONDAY, DECEMBER 19, 1910.

CITY POLICEMEN MURDERED BY ALIEN BURGLARS.

THE TERRIBLE MIDNIGHT SCENE IN EXCHANGE BUILDINGS, HOUNDSDITCH, WHERE THREE POLICE
WERE MURDERED AND TWO WOUNDED BY REVOLVER SHOTS FIRED BY FOREIGNERS, WHO ARE SUPP
TO HAVE BEEN ATTEMPTING A BURGLARY ON NEIGHBOURING PREMISES.

Sketched by a " Daily Graphic " Artist from materials supplied by an eye-witness of the outrage.

4 A contemporary artist's impression of the shootings in Exchange Buildings, Houndsditc

(a) Luba Milstein

(b) Peter Piaktow ('Peter the Painter')

(c) Osip Federoff

(d) Sara Trassjonsky

6 (a) Exchange
Buildings, looking
towards Cutler Stree
A policeman is
standing in the
doorway of No. 11,
on the left.
(Press Association)

(b) The bedroom at 59 Grove Street where Gardstein died

7 *(a)* Sidney Street the end of the siege

The kitchen where the body of Fritz Svaars was found *(Radio Times Hulton Picture Library)*

8 After the Revolution: Jacob Peters in 1930 *(United Press International)*

she knew; he was to tell him that Nina was ill and ask him to come at once. She was about to give him the name when she changed her mind and said that she would go herself. She confided that she was going to beg the doctor to give her an alibi and plead with him to say that she had been sleeping at his place for the past two or three nights. Certainly Nina felt the risk was justified as the doctor was the same one she had gone to for help for the dying Gardstein. Since he had not gone to the police as he had threatened, and had said nothing since, there was a slim chance that she could get him to agree to this. Also he was an old acquaintance, which was why she had gone to him for help in the first place. They had met three years before, when Nina was in domestic service in Dalston and used to do cleaning for the doctor's wife. Later, when she was self-employed as a cigarette-maker, she had gone to the doctor for orders, but after the first he had refused to give her any more as her prices were too steep. They had occasionally met since at Russian concerts. Four months before the murders the doctor, Mengle Freedman, had opened a practice at 54 Whitechapel Road, which was where Nina had gone for help and where she now went to see him.

When she appeared at the doctor's door, Nina later told Isaac Gordon, it seemed that he 'would have soon seen the devil as see her.' He told her to clear out and said that he would not do any of her dirty work, which would soon ruin his practice. He was badly frightened by her visit and later, when he was interviewed by the police, he stressed that Nina had not stayed with him at any time, either before or after the murders, and, like Dr Scanlon, was most anxious that his name should be kept out of the affair.

Nina went back to her lodgings equally frightened. She saturated the dark-blue blouse she had worn on the night of the murders with paraffin and set it alight. She also burned her black hat, but gave the feather trimming to Isaac Gordon, who asked for it, and the lining of her blue skirt, which was also consigned to the flames, to Fanny. She unwisely kept her blood-stained coat. She packed some clothes in a brown-paper parcel and made a present of the rest to Fanny Gordon. She was determined to escape. Next morning she said goodbye and tried to get away to Paris. She did not get very far. The same evening she returned in despair. She was terribly distressed and said that she had been followed everywhere by detectives. 'If I go to Russia I shall be killed and if I stop here I shall be hanged,' she moaned, and added fatalistically, 'What is to be, will be.'

Nor did the police succeed in lulling her suspicions by including the description of the woman they wanted for questioning on the reward posters. Five hundred pounds was offered for the capture of Fritz Svaars and Peter the Painter. The most likely claimant looked like being Nicholas Tomacoff. After bringing Federoff into the net, he was lodged in an hotel and his expenses paid for the next five weeks as he hunted for information. Everywhere he went he was accompanied by a policeman. From 24 December to 28 January the police showered him with gifts as the search switched between the West End and the East End. On 23 December the policemen bought him boots, a shirt, a collar and socks (15s 6d); on the 28th underpants, vest, socks and collar (8s 4d); on 2 January a hat and overcoat (14s 9d); on the fifth a new collar (6d); on 12 January more underclothes, handkerchiefs and collars (17s 3d). His five weeks' hotel-expenses cost £7 10s and there were other day-to-day expenses, fares, etc., as well. On 22 December he took them to 48 Turner Street where Fritz's cousin, Jacob Peters, was living. Tomacoff was not employed by the police on a day-to-day basis till the twenty-fourth; possibly he delayed giving them this information to demonstrate his usefulness. Fritz had, in fact, given him Peters' address some time before. The police were waiting in Peters' room when he came in. He was surrounded by armed police and searched. An interpreter, Casimir Pilenas, from the Thames Police Court, was with them as the arrested man apparently did not speak English, and spoke to him in Russian. He told him why he was being arrested. Immediately Peters answered, 'It is nothing to do with me. I can't help what my cousin Fritz has done.' His revolutionary experiences had taught him how to survive. Certainly he had no intention of hanging if he could shift the blame onto someone else.

Among the things the police had found in Grove Street was a small watercolour signed 'Yourka 16/12/10' and a slip of paper 'G. Dubof, 20 Galloway Road, Shepherd's Bush'. The house was watched, but the police made no contact until 22 December and then only because their hand was forced. From Tomacoff's description they thought that Yourka was another of Jacob Fogel's aliases. The Special Branch knew that he was on intimate terms with a man they knew only as Printer or Compositor, who in reality was Joseph; they knew that this man had worked under another name for a jeweller in Houndsditch. According to their information he had visited the Anarchist Club once or twice but was not known to have expressed any political opinions. They also knew that he was married to, or living with, a woman; but that was all. They did not know her name, which was Betsy Gershon, or where she lived, which was 100 Sidney Street.

Observation was kept on Dubof's address, but on 20 December there was an apparent leak of information. A journalist, George Mumford, working for the *Evening News*, was told by the news editor to go to the address and see what he could find out about a man called Yourka. As with Nina Vassilleva, the police had issued a description of Yourka and the others to lull suspicion. Mumford explained to the German landlady, Elsa Petter, that the police were offering a £500 reward for a man named Yourka and that she had a lodger of that name. The woman laughed and said that her husband had told her about it. 'He came home and said to my lodger, "Why, Yourka, they want you!"' He was nothing like the description, she said, but the journalist could judge for himself as Yourka was at the back of the house painting. She brought him through and as he spoke very little English she interpreted for him. Yourka Dubof apologised for his appearance. He was wearing a brown waistcoat and trousers and was without a collar and tie. The wanted man was described as aged twenty-one, 5 feet 8 inches in

height, of pale complexion, with dark-brown hair and heavy
moustache – the description, in fact, of Jacob Peters, although
because of lack of information this was not realised yet. Dubof,
in contrast, had a good colour, a small moustache and fair hair
which the journalist described as 'brown with a dash of bronze'.
He said he had only come from Switzerland three months
before and went to the Petters because his brother had once lived
with them. This was true. Dubof had left Perelman's lodging-
house in Wellesley Street at about the same time that Nina
Vassilleva had quarrelled with Fanny Perelman (see above,
page 42), which would be about March 1910. He had gone
to Switzerland and returned to England about the end of
September. He had been living at his present address since
then.

The landlady very largely monopolised the conversation.
When the journalist asked Yourka if he ever attended meetings
of Russians in London, she said that she had made it a condition of his coming to her house that he should not join any
Russian or political organisation. Dubof was obviously at a disadvantage in not speaking English, thought the journalist. He
seemed to want to give explanations but most of the time he
stood with his arms folded, looking at the landlady and then at
the reporter as if not knowing what to make of it. However, he
assured the journalist, with broken words and gestures, that
the names of Fritz and Peter the Painter meant nothing to him.
His evenings, he said, were spent talking with his landlord. The
journalist dictated a short paragraph which was published the
same day. It began 'Yourka – A common name leads to con-
fusion. The tale of a painter. Yourka is Russian for George.'

Next morning the journalist was interviewed by a detective,
and the following afternoon Detective Inspector Newell called
on Dubof and asked him to make a statement. Halfway through
he suggested that they should finish it at City Police headquarters. 'You make mistake. I will go with you,' Dubof said. Dubof
quickly admitted that he knew Fritz and Peter and had been at
59 Grove Street on the afternoon of the sixteenth. He knew that
Peter was a painter and had gone to him to find work as he had

been sacked on the Monday. He had taken a watercolour as a present.

He was the fifth prisoner in custody. Isaac Levy unhesitatingly identified him and Jacob Peters as the men he had seen dragging Gardstein out of Exchange Buildings, and who had threatened him with their pistols.

The hunt was intensified. For several days and nights the detectives had very little sleep. One detective's Christmas dinner was some bread and butter and tea in an alley down Petticoat Lane. Wensley and his men and City detectives combed all the lodging houses in the Whitechapel area, some sleeping 6–700 men nightly. On 23 December detectives followed Nina Vassilleva to St Paul's Cathedral to watch the funeral of the three murdered policemen. She bought a small black-and-silver memorial card, with wood-block portraits of the three men inside, which was later found in her handbag. The streets were choked with spectators. The Cathedral was crowded with people in black and dark blue. The Home Secretary, Winston Churchill, and Mrs Churchill were followed by the Lord Mayor in his state robe of black and gold, preceded by the Black Mourning Sword and accompanied by the Sheriffs and Aldermen in scarlet gowns trimmed with crêpe. As the three coffins were carried into the Cathedral the voices of the choir floated down the long nave. In front of the coffins was carried the great gilt cross; the coffins were placed on catafalques in front of the choir by the opening to the crypt. On each coffin was the dead man's helmet, Bentley's having a hole in the rim where the bullet had crossed his face.

Before the funeral, photographs were taken of the murdered policemen. As was then customary with mortuary photographs the corpses were dressed in their clothes – in this case their uniforms and greatcoats buttoned to the neck – and strapped to stretchers and photographed against the wall with their helmets on their heads. Photographs were also taken of Gardstein. He lay on a mortuary slab but his head was propped up on a block and the eyelids propped open so that a lifelike portrait could be taken for the poster. His identity was still uncertain and it was hoped that somebody would make a positive identification from the poster; it was marked 'Portrait and description of the dead murderer'.

Jacob Kempler (see above, page 42), passing by Arbour Square police station a few days later, recognised the dead man from the picture as his lodger 'P. Morin'. The discovery of Gardstein's lodgings at 44 Gold Street were widely publicised as 'The Stepney Bomb Factory'. In his room, it was said, were 'materials suitable for the manufacture of bombs, a supply of deadly acids, piles of cartridges sufficient to kill crowds, and a quantity of anarchist literature'.

As the investigations gathered momentum, Tomacoff began to lose some of his usefulness. In the immigrant community he was already being pointed out as the informer helping the police. When the police were finally given the whereabouts of Fritz and Joseph the source was not Tomacoff but someone completely unknown. The informant came to City Police headquarters in the late evening of New Year's Day. It was snowing heavily. Only scribbled notes were kept of the conversation. Fritz Svaars and Joseph, he said, were hiding in 100 Sidney Street with a woman lodger, Betsy Gershon.

Who was the informer? The police kept his name secret, but in the pencil notes that survive he referred to his cousin's lodgings in 83 Nelson Street. It might have been possbile to trace the name of the tenant from the rate books or electoral rolls, but the former were destroyed in the war and, as the tenant was an immigrant and had not been long resident, he was excluded from the latter. Other trails have proved equally fruitless. But we do know from the notes that the informer went to 100 Sidney Street at 2 p.m. the next day to see the two men and incredibly, in evidence given to an investigating committee some months later, the landlord described not only his visit but the man himself, although he did not know his name. He said he opened the door to a gentleman 'who wore a cap and a Chester and boots with leggings on, but he had a little parcel under his arm;

it was simply like an umbrella, but it was a long thing, and it was white and covered with American cloth carried under his arm. He wanted to speak to Mrs Gershon who called down, "Mrs Fleischmann let him up, he is a photographer"; and I let him up, and he might have been there from a quarter past two till about ten minutes to three when he came down . . . ' Almost certainly the informer was the gang's old landlord from Great Garden Street and Wellesley Street, Charles Perelman, who still earned his living as a photograph-enlarger.

Mrs Gershon had come to Perelman on the Saturday, New Year's Eve, and told him that Fritz and Joseph had come to her on 17 December asking for the address of two men called Abraham and Pavell who might help them. This was the first surprise. If this Pavell was Pavell Molchanoff, why hadn't they gone with Peter the Painter to Molchanoff's on the night of the Houndsditch murders (see above, page 83)? Perelman did not know Pavell's address but told her that if she called back two hours later at 8.30 p.m. he might have been able to get it. He said that he would do anything for the two men. When she returned he told her that he had been unsuccessful. She then asked, 'Can I speak openly?' Perelman took her into another room and she told him that the two men had been living with her since the murders but she was afraid that they would be discovered and wanted to find them another address. Perelman told her that he would find rooms and arranged to meet her the next day at 1.30 p.m. She then said that the best thing he could do was to go and see them.

Next day they met at 1.45 p.m. and Perelman accompanied her to 100 Sidney Street. The landlady let them in and, while Mrs Gershon kept watch on the stairs, Perelman spoke to Fritz and Joseph. They stood the whole time with their hands in their overcoat pockets. Perelman told them that he could find them rooms if they had money. Fritz said that he had £20 and would like a room in Dalston. As Perelman was leaving Fritz gave him a letter to post.

The letter, which Perelman handed to the police, was enclosed in two envelopes with both addresses written in red ink; the outer envelope was addressed in Russian 'To Jahn Ludman, No. 64 Pastbischna Street, Libau, Kourland' and the inner in Lettish marked 'Please hand it to J. F. Luaram No. 8 Boschu Street, Libau'. The letter was written in Lettish in black ink. Fritz explained how he was planning to leave for Australia with three friends between 7 and 10 January, by which time his wife should have joined him. He had sufficient money for the voyage. He explained how Gardstein had borrowed money from him and promised to repay it with interest but how he had been brought instead, wounded but alive, to his lodgings by two friends and how Fritz himself had been forced to flee because there was a risk that he might be caught and made to talk. He narrated the rest of the night's events: how he had ordered the girls to burn the house if Gardstein died, and how they had been arrested. His *zaineeks teie*, as he called Luba, did not know if he and Joseph were at home or not and the only thing that was certain if he was caught was that he would be hanged. Therefore he was ready either to defend or to shoot himself.

Perelman said that he had arranged for the two men to have the back room on the second floor at his cousin's house, 83 Nelson Street, and had passed this information to Mrs Gershon earlier that evening. She had since told him that they would move between 5 and 6 p.m. the next day.

Wensley was hurriedly called to City Police headquarters at Old Jewry for a conference the next morning, and a plan was made to trap the two men in the street. Two large horse-drawn waggons with armed police inside drove into the street late on Monday afternoon and waited for the men to leave. Nothing happened. Shortly after 9 p.m. Mrs Gershon went to Perelman's house once more and told him that Fritz would not leave now until nine o'clock the next night, and Joseph would want a coded reply from Fritz that he was safe before he left 100 Sidney Street to join him.

VII

The Siege of Sidney Street

A BLEARY-EYED Wensley was still working at Leman Street police station when the telephone rang just before midnight. The voice at the other end of the line was Superintendent Ottaway's and he sounded anxious. 'We don't like the look of things,' he said. 'The informant is not all that can be desired and seems shifty. It will never do to let these people slip through our fingers now – there's no guarantee that they will move tomorrow night. We propose, if you agree, to act tonight.'

Wensley agreed. As soon as it was daylight it would be impossible to conceal the light scattering of detectives watching the house and, in such a sensitive area, this information might quickly be passed to the two gunmen. He offered to bring the rest of his detectives but Ottaway thought that by themselves they might not be enough, and proposed bringing a stiffener of uniformed men. As this meant bringing men from another force and from another police district into H Division, Wensley told him to bring his men to Arbour Square police station while he sent Sergeant Leeson with a message to the home of Divisional Superintendent Mulvaney in Commercial Road telling him what was happening.

Ottaway swung into action and ordered the single men out. Shivering in their blue great-coats they straggled through the empty streets, with their faces turned away from the bitterly cold wind which by now was gusting sheets of snow and rain. As yet they did not know what had happened, but when they

heard that the married men were to be left behind they realised
that there was likely to be some shooting and guessed the rest.
At Arbour Square police station they stamped their feet and
tried to get warm again while in a nearby office the officers held
a hurried consultation.

The meeting began at 12.45 a.m. None of the officers, including Wensley, had an intimate knowledge of the locality
and it was left to one of Wensley's detectives, Sergeant Girdler,
to brief them. Snatching up a piece of paper he began to draw
as they leant over his shoulder. Superintendent Mulvaney turned
up the gas flares to give him more light. Sergeant Girdler scored
the paper with two parallel lines to indicate Sidney Street, which
runs between the Mile End Road and Commercial Road. He
then blocked off a square on the right side of the road. All the
houses in this square faced outwards, and in the centre were the
yards. The streets going round the square, starting with Lindley
Street in the north, were Richardson Street, Hawkins Street
and Sidney Street. The house where the two men were hiding
was part of a block of ten four-storey houses built in 1900. Not
only were they bigger than the usual grey two-storey houses in
the area but they had facing of red brick and were grandilo-
quently known, after the landlord, as Charley Martin's Man-
sions. The house they wanted was next but one to the surgery
on the corner of Hawkins Street.

The three superintendents and Wensley then discussed ways
and means of getting the gunmen out. Even as they made their
plans they were uncomfortably aware that there was no
guarantee that the murderers had in fact been located, or that
they were the right men. John Stark, one of the City Police
superintendents, spoke for them all when he said, 'This whole
operation could make us a laughing stock.' As they talked, Superintendent Mulvaney ordered that a hundred of his own men
should be mustered in the parade room to match the City's
hundred men. They finally agreed to Wensley's suggestion that
men should be placed in the houses on either side of the house,
in case they should try to escape by breaking through the adjoining walls, and that it should be covered front and rear from

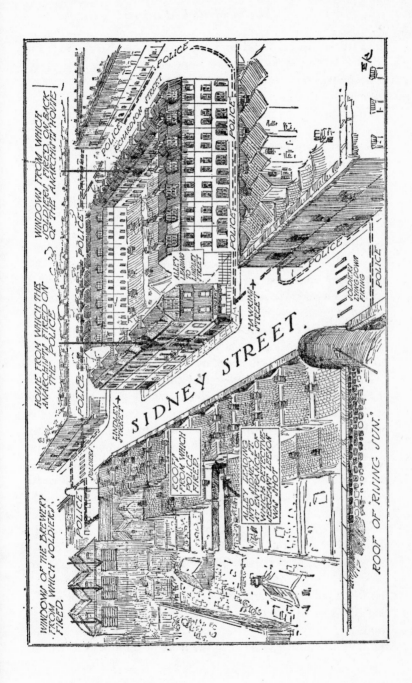

the yards at the back and from the houses opposite. As Sergeant Girdler knew the locality and some of the people who lived there he was sent with twelve detectives, carrying revolvers and truncheons, to Sidney Street to make the preliminary moves.

Sergeant Girdler divided them into parties of four and left two at the corner of Richardson Street and Hawkins Street. The third party went with him to 3 Hawkins Street where he knocked on the window of the ground-floor flat of Mrs Rubenoff. She opened her door and then went straight back to her room without saying a word. Girdler crept through the passage with the four men and in the back yard directed them to climb over a low wall into the yard of 1 Hawkins Street, which was directly opposite the back of 100 Sidney Street. Having posted them he returned to the corner of Hawkins Street and knocked on the door of No. 98, which was a doctor's surgery. He posted four more men in the yard, and repeated the same operation again at No. 102 with the last four. Soon after 2 a.m., the rear of the house was completely sealed off. At the same time the whole block was cordoned off with 200 men to cut off all chance of escape.

In the meantime, Wensley and the City officers had been considering their next move, which was to place armed men in the houses and shuttered shops immediately opposite. Some of the City men were armed with Morris-tube rifles, and others with revolvers which were so antiquated that most had to be reloaded after each shot. Wensley asked George Weston, one of his sergeants, if there was any chance of getting into the wood yard next to Cohen's the chemist at No. 109 on the other side of the street. Weston said, 'Yes – I know Cohen well.' He crept across the street and tapped at the door but got no answer. He then tried the door of the yard but that too was locked. 'Frank,' he whispered, as Sergeant Girdler slipped in beside him, 'can we get this wicket door of the yard open?' Girdler grinned and felt in his pocket; within minutes he had opened the door with a skeleton key. He crept back to his post in Lindley Street as more men moved silently into the yard. From the yard some of the uniformed men broke into the back of the house and woke the couple sleeping in the bedroom overlooking the street. There was a hurried explanation, and as the startled owner and his wife dressed and hurried downstairs they watched with dismay as more policemen trampled into their bedroom and trod snow and water into their fur carpets. The policemen positioned themselves with their rifles behind the lace curtains and partly barricaded the window with the mattress which they yanked off the bed. More armed men were positioned in the shop doorways facing the house and, shortly after 3 a.m., the house was completely surrounded.

Wensley suggested to the officers, 'If I were you, I would get into No. 102 and find out from the occupier the character of the landlord and landlady of No. 100. If they are respectable we shall be doing a good thing if we can quietly get them out.' Detectives were already in the yard of No. 102 but although the landlady, Mrs Bluestein, had co-operated, somewhat unwillingly, with the police so far she bristled at the mention of her next-door neighbour, Mrs Fleishmann, with whom she was on extremely bad terms, and Wensley had great difficulty in finding out what he wanted to know. Eventually he got from her a grudging admission that she was a respectable woman, but when Wensley explained that he proposed waking her up and bringing her into the house Mrs Bluestein, after expressing her disapproval with considerable force, went to bed rather than encounter her neighbour. The Fleishmanns, Wensley had learned, slept in the front room on the ground floor and, taking with him the Jewish interpreter the City officers had brought with them, he rapped on the window shutters of the house next door. Rebecca Fleishmann half rolled over and listened.

'That's the milkman,' she said, nudging her husband. Samuel grunted and snuggled deeper into the feather mattress. 'I won't get up,' he muttered. 'You go as you arrange for the milkman.' Rebecca did not waste any time arguing as their youngest daughter, Leah, was asleep in the same room, and crept over to the window. 'I don't want any milk,' she hissed.

'No, not the milkman,' she heard someone say. The interpreter, Henry Wagner, spoke in Yiddish. 'It is the police.'

Rebecca crept back to her bed and pummelled her husband awake. 'It is not the milkman, it is somebody else,' she said doubtfully. 'Get up.'

Samuel staggered irritably to the window. Like his wife he thought that the time was about 7 a.m. 'We don't want any milk,' he shouted.

'I am not a milkman – I am from the police,' Wagner persisted. Samuel snapped up the blind and stared through the glass. 'I don't believe you,' he said. Wagner held up a truncheon. 'Don't be afraid – come out,' he pleaded.

Samuel told his wife to come with him. Mrs Fleishmann in particular was disturbed at seeing so many policemen; she was so distressed that in her haste she did not put her stockings on. Wensley asked how many lodgers there were. She told him that there was an old couple named Clements in the ground floor back room next to her bedroom; in the first-floor front room there was another lodger David Schiemann, his wife and four children. The Fleishmanns' twins were in the back room on the first floor. On the second floor the front room was let to Mrs Gershon, and Mr Fleishmann used the back room as a stock room. He also used the large attic as a tailor's shop.

They asked her about Mrs Gershon. Mrs Fleishmann described her as a tall, thin woman with glasses. No, she didn't know if there were any strange men with her. Wensley then turned to her husband and told him that he must go and fetch Mrs Gershon down. Samuel Fleishmann was horrified. He was a very nervous man by nature and seeing so many policemen had frightened him still more. 'Not for £1000,' he said. He explained later, 'I can tell you, if I see so many officers in the night time, nobody would be fool enough to go upstairs.' Wensley tried Mrs Fleishmann again. He had heard that she was a respectable woman and would not tolerate two men living with a woman in her house. He suggested that she went upstairs and saw for herself if this were so. He again met with a stubborn refusal. 'I would not do it for £5000 nor let my husband do it.' Wensley's manner changed. He inferred that both of them knew something and ignored their strenuous denials that they didn't.

Samuel Fleishmann was coughing badly and Wensley suggested, 'Go up and ask Mrs Gershon to come down as your husband has been taken very bad and you want her to help you.' Rebecca said nothing – but went.

The stairs were dark, but she had lived in the house for eleven years and knew the way. She knocked on Mrs Gershon's door. There was no light under the door so she knocked again. To her chagrin the stock-room door behind her opened and Mrs Gershon came out barefoot and wearing only a petticoat. For a moment Mrs Fleishmann's outraged sense of propriety got the better of her, but she recovered sufficiently to explain that her husband was very ill.

'Give me a little help,' she said.

The two women crept downstairs and as they reached the first-floor landing Mrs Gershon was seized and carried next door. She indignantly denied having anyone in her room until Wensley told her that he was going up there to see for himself. If he was killed, he said, she would be hanged as she knew who they were. She then said that there was a cousin of her husband up there and only reluctantly admitted the presence of a second man. They had called the previous evening, she lied, and refused to go. When she insisted they leave they had made her take off her skirt and boots so that she could not run away, and had forced her to sleep on an old sofa in the stock room. So the two men were still there. A coat was flung over Mrs Gershon's shoulders and she was taken to City Police headquarters.

The police now had a problem. If they went into the house they could not, according to law, open fire until they had been fired on first; this would put them at an impossible disadvantage. In addition, the staircase was narrow ($3\frac{1}{2}$ feet wide), with a bend at the top, which would make the operation extremely hazardous.

Superintendent Mulvaney later explained:

The measurements of the passage and staircase will show how futile any attempt to storm or rush the place would have been, with two men ... dominating the position from the head of the stairs and where, to an extent, they were well under cover from fire. The passage at one discharge would have been blocked by fallen men; had any even reached the stairs, it could only have been by climbing over the bodies of their comrades, when they would stand little chance of getting further; had they even done this the two desperadoes could retreat up the staircase to the first and second storey, on each of which, what had occurred below would have been repeated.

They decided that it would be best to bring everyone out of the house and then wait for daylight before making their next move. Mrs Fleishmann brought out her children, and then went back again to the first floor, woke Mrs Schiemann and told her to get up quietly. She took the two babies and the Schiemanns' two other children safely downstairs. Old Mr and Mrs Clements on the ground floor were more of a problem. She was quickly persuaded to leave, but her ninety-year-old husband obstinately refused to move out of his bed; to make things more difficult, he was stone deaf. Fleishmann tried to frighten him by saying there were burglars in the house, but the old man only snuggled deeper into his bed of which, said Mrs Fleishmann later, he was very fond. About this time somebody blew a police whistle, and when Fleishmann came to the street door and told the waiting policeman that the old man did not want to come out someone growled, 'Put him in his trousers.' The interpreter went back with him and together they forced the whining old man into his clothes and then struggled out of the house with him on their backs. Nothing was to be gained by gagging him as he was the last to leave. The two inspectors, Wensley and Thompson, propped the street door open and the first-floor lodger, David Schiemann, turned up the gas. The policemen in the house opposite clutched their rifles; they stared intently at the empty hall and lower staircase, and waited.

Slowly it began to get light. The policemen cordoning off the block were tired, hungry and very cold. The snow was turning to slush, but the wind had not dropped. At the back of the house, the detectives pulled their caps down further over their eyes and rested their arms on the chest-high walls with their revolvers numbly clutched between their stiff fingers. In Hawkins Street a new baker's shop was opening. Three men and several boys had been hired to hand out 20,000 leaflets, but only three of them had turned up. The leaflets were to publicise a brass band which had been specially hired for the grand opening and, at 7 a.m., policemen and neighbours alike were treated to the band's opening piece from the top floor of the shop. A policeman told them to stop playing but the baker ignored him; the band, in fact, went on playing for an hour.

The streets were still largely deserted, but people were just beginning to hover behind the police cordon. At about 7.30 there was another hurried conference in the wood yard and it was decided to try to attract the wanted men's attention. Sergeant Weston ran across the road and banged furiously on the still-open door of the house and then ran back. Then Wensley asked his men to throw some pebbles at the second-floor windows. They spattered against the glass, still without producing a reaction. Then somebody picked up a brick to throw and, as it was flung at the same window, a pane of glass in the window of the floor below shattered and half a dozen shots sprayed the group of policemen at the entrance to the yard. One bullet passed through somebody's bowler hat. Sergeant Leeson yelled, 'Jack, I am hit', and ran into the yard with Sergeant Weston behind him. Shots were spurting from the stones in the yard as they ran for cover and the gates were slammed behind them. Leeson collapsed against the rear of a van as Wensley ripped open his shirt and coat which were soaked with blood. Wensley had little doubt that the Sergeant was dying. Leeson himself thought so too. He is recorded as saying melodramatically, 'Mr Wensley, I am dying. They have shot me through the heart. Goodbye. Give my love to the children. Bury me at Putney.' Wensley pressed his hand. 'We will be with you to the last,' he said.

Superintendent Mulvaney ran upstairs to the bedroom where the City men were positioned with their rifles to find out if they had seen the men who had fired the shots or had returned

fire. They had not, but as he stood talking bullets started rico-
cheting off the walls and smashing the glass chandelier. He went
downstairs again and sat by Leeson who had been carried into
the kitchen.

Someone ran across the street to the corner surgery next to
the besieged house and brought back Dr Krestin but Leeson,
even though he thought he was dying, waved him away as he
doubted his medical qualifications. In the meantime Louis
Levy, who kept his coffee stall in the yard and who had been
trapped by the shooting, climbed over the roofs to fetch Dr
Nelson Johnstone from his surgery in the Mile End Road. Dr
Johnstone arrived about twenty minutes after the detective had
been shot. A bullet whistled passed him as he crossed Sidney
Street. Once in the yard Levy pointed to an outhouse and told
him that he would have to climb over it and the adjoining walls
to reach the wounded man. Johnstone handed him one of his
bags and together the two men climbed onto the roof with the
help of a ladder, crawled along the coping and eventually
reached the wood yard. Leeson was lying on a couch in the
kitchen. His coat, waistcoat and shirt were open. The bullet
wound was level with the left nipple and about two inches in
towards the centre of the chest. Johnstone was about to probe
the wound when the detective said, 'It is not there, doctor, it
has gone out the other side.' Johnstone pulled back Leeson's
coat and found another wound about four and a half inches
beyond and about three-eighths of an inch below the right nipple.
The bullet had apparently struck the rib, passed under the breast
bone, glanced along another rib and passed out at the right side.
Leeson was spitting blood and in a state of total collapse. 'Someone take this,' he said, remembering the revolver in his right-
hand pocket. The doctor took it and gingerly placed it in his
hip pocket to give to Wensley. He plugged the wounds and
revived the wounded man with a large dose of brandy.

It was vital to get Leeson to hospital. The only way was over
the yard outhouses at the rear backing onto Mann & Crossman's
brewery. Wensley scrambled over and came back with a
stretcher, which was hauled into the yard. He then got a van in

the yard, pushed it up against a dung pit and placed a ladder at
a slant from the van to the outhouses, which were about fourteen feet high. Leeson was brought out on the stretcher, lifted
from the ground to the van, then dragged across the ladder and
onto the roof of the outhouse. Wensley and the others on the
roof were hampered by a blinding fall of sleet but had so far
been unobserved by the two gunmen although they were now
above the level of the gateway. Suddenly a man's helmet
appeared; he was mounting a ladder from the brewery side of
the wall. Wensley shouted at him to get back, but it was too
late. Shots began to smash against the wet and slippery tiles.
A bullet grazed Dr Johnstone's forehead; he shouted to Wensley
to lie down. Wensley flung himself forward onto the broken
tiles and for about ten minutes he and Leeson, who was still
lying helpless on the stretcher, were exposed to the constant
stream of fire. Eventually Leeson, unwilling to let anyone else
expose themselves to the fusillade, rolled off the stretcher and
over to the wall and was helped down to the safety of the
brewery yard. Wensley now found himself a solitary target on
the roof just as the gunmen were getting their range; the bullets
were coming unpleasantly close. His only chance of safety was
the gutter of the outhouse which was apparently shielded by the
ridge of the wall. He lay at full length in an inch or so of sleet
and water; he was frozen stiff, and the slightest movement was
greeted with a shower of bullets. It never occurred to him,
he reflected later, that he could have escaped by loosening the
tiles near him and dropping through the roof to the interior
of the outhouse. He was trapped for half an hour. Meanwhile, a rumour that he had been shot was steadily gaining
circulation.

The shooting had been going on for about an hour now and
it was clear that the gunmen dominated the situation with their
superior fire-power. Stark and Mulvaney conferred again and
guessed that the two men were using Mauser pistols, which were
far superior to the police's Morris-tube rifles. In a lull in the
firing which released Wensley, they scrambled over the outhouses into the brewery and tried unsuccessfully to telephone

Scotland Yard. They hurried back to Arbour Square police station. This time they were more successful. Mulvaney spoke to the Commissioner, Major Woodhouse, and asked for the necessary authority to bring in troops from the Tower of London.

Woodhouse could not give this authority without consulting the Home Office, who passed on his request to the Home Secretary, Winston Churchill. Churchill was in his bath when he was surprised by an urgent knocking at the door. 'There is a message from the Home Office on the telephone. Absolutely immediate.' Dripping wet and shrouded in a towel, he hurried to the telephone and was told what had happened, and that authority was requested to send for troops to arrest or kill them. He at once authorised the police to use whatever force was necessary and in about twenty minutes was dressed and at the Home Office. There he found that no further information was available other than that the house had been surrounded and the anarchists were firing in all directions. No one knew how many anarchists there were or what other measures were to be taken. In the circumstances he thought it advisable, and his advisers concurred, that he should see for himself what was going on. Later he admitted 'that convictions of duty were supported by a strong sense of curiosity which perhaps it would have been well to keep in check'.*

Armed with the Home Secretary's authority, Superintendent Mulvaney hurried to the Tower, stopping only to tell Mrs Leeson that her husband had been wounded but was all right, and spoke to the officer commanding the Scots Guards. After telephoning the G.O.C. he was told he could have the help of Lieutenant Ross, two non-commissioned officers and seventeen men; they accompanied him back to Sidney Street, arriving shortly after 10 a.m. The soldiers in their heavy grey coats and their distinctive caps, with the diced cap-bands, halted in Richardson Street. Three went with Superintendent Stark to Mann & Crossman's brewery and climbed the high building which they used as a bottling store. The upper part of the

* Winston S. Churchill, *Thoughts and Adventures*.

building, which was at right angles to Sidney Street and over-looked the wood yard, had three large slatted windows. Through the slats the soldiers could just see the attic and second-floor windows of 100 Sidney Street. Stark pointed out the house to them by indicating a broken chimney pot which was directly in their line of fire. Within minutes they had shattered it, and were firing round after round into the upper windows of the house. Thus the gunmen were forced to move down to the first and ground-floor windows where they were exposed to an equally devastating fire from another party of soldiers, now occupying the windows formerly manned by the police. Superintendent Mul-vaney posted three soldiers at the corner of Oxford Street and Sidney Street, two at the end of Hawkins Street, two at the corner of Lindley Street and three at the Mile End Road end of Sidney Street. Between 11 and 12 noon some sixty policemen from the surrounding divisions came armed with revolvers, and a gun-smith also arrived with shotguns and ammunition; these were handed out to policemen with military experience.

Since daylight there had been a steady stream of rumours of fighting in the East End, and sightseers had followed the small squads of policemen they saw marching through White-chapel to Sidney Street. Throughout the morning the cordons had to be strengthened again and again to keep the crowds out of range of the Mausers, which were sighted up to a thousand yards. They watched awe-struck as the soldiers from the brewery tower kept up a sustained fire. The snow turned to a drizzle, and by mid-morning the street was lit up with a watery brightness. Every now and again there would be a puff of smoke and a spit of flame from the house and an answering rattle of shots from the soldiers' Lee Enfields. Some of the policemen had heard a rumour that Leeson was dead and were in a frenzy to rush the house; it was only with the greatest difficulty that they were restrained. One detective was foolhardy enough to run down the street with a rifle and smash the windows on the ground floor; he ran back again to great cheers from the crowd. Similarly a postman insisted on delivering letters to within a few doors of the house, and an old woman close by came to her door at frequent periods throughout the morning and, arms folded, calmly watched the pistol flashes and bullets streaking the red façade.

From the roof of the Rising Sun public house the *Daily Chronicle* reporter had a bird's-eye view.

At both ends of Sidney Street the Scots Guards were in position, taking cover behind the angle of the houses. Around them were groups of policemen in uniform armed with shotguns, and numbers of plain clothes detectives with heavy revolvers. In the shadow of doorways and archways men crouched down with barrels of rifles and pistols pointed towards the house next to the doctor's surgery, with its shattered window-panes and broken brickwork. Looking down into the backyards of the houses opposite Martins-buildings, I could see soldiers and armed policemen moving about, climbing over fences, and getting up tall ladders, so that they could fire between the chimney pots.

On the roof of a great brewery on the same side of the way as the Rising Sun public-house were scores of the workpeople, and as far as the eye could see across the sloping roofs, the chimney-pots and parapets, the sky-line was black with heads, while in the streets below, as far as a quarter of a mile away, there were vast and tumultous crowds, kept back by lines of mounted policemen. The voices of those many thousands came up to me in great murmurous gusts, like the roar of wild beasts in a jungle. It seemed as if the whole of London had poured into Whitechapel and Stepney to watch one of the most deadly and thrilling dramas that has ever happened in the great city within living memory.

But my eyes were now fixed upon one building, and no other impression could find a place in my mind. The anarchists' had the horrible fascination of a house of death. Bullets were raining upon it. As I looked I saw how they spat at the walls, how they ripped splinters from the door, how they made neat grooves as they burrowed into the red bricks, or chipped off corners of them. The noise of battle was tremendous and almost continuous. The heavy barking reports of Army rifles were followed by the sharp and lighter cracks of pistol shots. Some of the weapons had a shrill singing noise, and others were like children's pop guns. Most terrible and deadly in sound was the rapid fire of the Scots Guards, shot speeding on shot, as though a Gatling gun were at work. Then there would come a sudden lull, as though a bugle had sounded 'Cease fire', followed by a silence, intense and strange, after the ear-splitting din.

It reopened again when a few moments later there came the spitting fire of an automatic pistol from the house next to the surgery. From my vantage point I could see how the assassins changed the position from which they fired. The idea that only two men were concealed within that arsenal seemed disproved by the extreme rapidity with which their shots came from one floor and another. As I watched, gripped by the horror and drama of it, I saw a sharp stabbing flash break through the garret window. The man's weapon must have been over the edge of the window-sill. He emptied his magazine, spitting out the shots at the house opposite, from which picked marksmen of the Scots Guards replied with instant volleys. A minute later by my watch shots began to pour through the second floor window, and before the echo of them had died away there was a fusillade from the ground floor.

So this amazing duel went on, as a distinct clock chimed the quarters and half hours. From 11 o'clock until 12.30 there were not scores or hundreds of shots fired, but thousands. It seemed that the assassins had an almost inexhaustible supply of ammunition.

At about noon the Home Secretary's car was stopped on the fringes of the crowd. The crowd, thought Churchill, as he got out, were not particularly friendly. There were several cries of 'Oo let 'em in?' in allusion to the Liberal Government's refusal to restrict alien immigration. With the help of the police he pushed his way through the cordon to the corner of Hawkins Street and Sidney Street. Almost at once the situation became embarrassing. He had no wish to take personal control but his position of authority inevitably attracted to itself direct responsibility. He saw that he would have done much better to have remained in his office but it was impossible to get into his car and drive away while matters were so uncertain, and – he wrote later – so 'extremely interesting'. Anxious to have a better view of the house he crossed the road and sheltered in the doorway of a warehouse.

'Plans were now made to storm the building from several sides at once,' he later wrote.* 'One party, emerging from the next-door house, was to rush the front door and charge up the stairs; another party of police and soldiers would break into the second floor at the back through a window; a third, smashing in the roof, would leap down on the assassins from above.' All of these plans, with the exception of the first, were hopelessly impractical, and on Churchill's suggestion a search was made of the foundries in the neighbourhood for a steel plate or shield which would protect them if they rushed the stairs. Such a plan could only have resulted in some loss of life and fortunately was never tried. At about 1 p.m. there was a shout from the crowd followed by a few moments of silence in which not a single shot was fired. From the garret window a thin haze of bluish smoke curled up towards the roof.

'The house is on fire! They will be smoked out like rats or burnt alive!' As the minutes passed the smoke increased in volume. The wind was not strong enough to carry it away and soon the whole roof was shrouded in clouds of grey wispy smoke. Soon there was another shout: 'The second floor is alight! They must surrender or suffocate.'

Gradually the smoke became thicker. Slowly it funnelled through the shattered windows and rolled in billowing clouds out through the front and the back of the house and gathered over the roof like an angry storm-cloud. Presently scraps of torn paper and the ashes of burnt paper floated out and mingled with the smoke. From the roof of the Rising Sun a reporter could see a gas jet burning steadily in the first-floor room and guessed that the men had deliberately set fire to the house before attempting to escape. The most likely route was through the back of the house where earlier the waiting detectives had seen two men come to an upstairs window. One of them was carrying two pistols which he fired simultaneously through the window; minutes later a defective cartridge containing a very

* Churchill, *Thoughts and Adventures*.

small charge of powder jammed in the rifling of one of the Mausers putting it out of action. As the thousands of pieces of black and white paper fluttered like butterflies over the heads of the crowd the soldiers increased their volume of fire. But the men inside were still alive. Once, one of them leaned too far through the window. Instantly he became the target for concentrated fire; it seems likely, from subsequent evidence, that he was killed at that time by a bullet through the brain. At about 1.30 p.m. the first tongues of flame flickered through the attic windows and licked the roof. Lower down there were still the black, heavy billowing clouds of smoke. Suddenly there was a gasp of horror from the watching thousands. It looked as if a smoke-charred figure was climbing through the first-floor window and standing huddled up on the sill outside. Again there was a concentrated burst of firing and then the 'figure' fluttered in the wind, the smoke drifted away and it was seen that it was only a torn and charred curtain. Once more there was the short, sharp flash of shooting from the burning house.

The houses on either side were now evacuated in case they should catch fire, or in case the gunmen should try to escape by breaking through the wall. The Fire Brigade stood by to put out the flames; they had been dissuaded from advancing on the house only on the personal intervention of Churchill himself. His orders were to let the house burn. 'Flames now burst out in a fury,' wrote the *Daily Chronicle* reporter.

The garret was burning like matchwood. From my position on the Rising Sun I could hear the roar of those fire-demons. In another quarter of an hour they had burned their way through the topmost rafters; with a great uproar they surged skywards and made a fiery crown upon the roof. By this time the first floor also was a seething furnace of flame. The angry tongues were thrust out three yards from the gaping jaws of that awful house.

About quarter of an hour passed and then the flames broke through the roof and curled about the gables. The crackle and the roar steadily increased and with a great crash the roof fell in, exposing the charred and burning ribs. From the first-floor window great tongues of flame shot out against the bullet-scarred walls. Only on the ground floor could anyone survive; Again there was a tremendous crash as another part of the house collapsed. 'The first floor fell in with a shock of splintered wood and cracking iron, and again a pillar of fire with a whirlwind of dancing sparks rose high into the clear sky, where the winter sun was shining.' Moments before the first floor collapsed a gust of wind lifted the smoke from the ground-floor window and the watchers opposite looked into the blazing inferno that had once been the Fleishmanns' bedroom. They distinctly saw a man lying on the bed with his face buried in a pillow and the flames streaking up the walls and floor about him. Then the smoke rolled back, obliterating him completely, and the ceiling collapsed.

Blazing timbers were flung into the street, masses of masonry crashed down, fiery splinters, like shooting stars, were hurtled a hundred yards or more. Broken glass fell upon the pavement again and again with a dreadful sound of destruction. And into all this turmoil and fury there poured a terrific artillery of shots. The soldiers were volleying now from every window and every roof on the opposite side of Sidney Street, and their shots had thunderous echoes, for other soldiers and many police were firing into the back of the blazing house from the . . . yard.

Detectives with their revolvers ready walked slowly towards the house and re-entered the houses on either side to make sure the men had not broken through the walls. A whistle blew and the firemen walked cautiously down the street, their helmets gleaming in the dull afternoon light, with soldiers and more armed policemen. A detective walked up to the door and, lifting his foot high, kicked it open. As it swung back a great belch of flame roared out but it was clear that nobody could still be alive. Within minutes the hoses were pumping great jets of water into the house and soon there were only great clouds of black smoke left hovering over the charred ruins, the twisted metal and the crumbling walls.

On the way back to the Yard, where poached egg and whisky were waiting, the refrain of an old comic song kept running through one detective's head: 'I say what a day we are having, my boys! I say what a day we are having!'

VIII

Headless Bodies

ONCE the front door had been kicked open the firemen soon got into the building. As heavy jets of water were poured into the back of the house, they dragged their hoses into the passage and quickly doused the flames. After half an hour they began to search through the flooded debris, which they threw into the yard. Almost immediately a bulky mass was noticed about three feet from the fire-place. The head was missing and there appeared to be just the stump of the neck and the bone of an arm protruding. As the firemen pulled away more debris they saw that most of the clothes had been burnt off and that the legs had disappeared. The body itself was sitting in a half-upright position which suggested that it had fallen through from one of the upper rooms. A fireman started digging with a spade in the centre of the room and began to work his way towards the window; two feet from the wall he found a skull cap and brains with 'only about an inch of stuff underneath the brain pan'.

As they were working the upper floor and part of the side wall collapsed on top of them. Five firemen were dragged out of the rubble, with bleeding hands and faces, and taken to the London Hospital where one of them later died from his injuries. The search was soon resumed. The charred body was bundled into a coffin, which was tied up with string, and taken to Horseferry Branch Road mortuary.

It was nearly 8 p.m. before the firemen found the second

body lying on its left side in the back room. One of them caught hold of an arm, but the hand and wrist were missing and a small piece of skin about 6 inches long came away in his hand. Carefully he scraped away some of the rubble and uncovered a pistol apparently lying on the man's back about halfway between the neck and the hip. The police surgeon, Charles Grant, caught hold of the charred arms sticking up through the ashes and pulled on the bones; the body rose up to meet him but the head was missing. Most of the body had been destroyed by fire but in places it had been protected by falling debris. A brain pan was handed to him and some pieces of feet and limbs in a towel. This second body was also taken away for post-mortem examination. The firemen later found two wigs belonging to old Mrs Clements, which promptly led to rumours that Fritz and Joseph had tried to escape as women.

Most newspapers correctly assumed that the bodies were those of Fritz Svaars and Joseph, but others were beginning to find the plethora of names confusing. Joseph was wrongly identified with Yoska alias Jacob Fogel or Vogel, and the *Daily Mail* completely baffled its readers by claiming that 'Mouremtzoff alias Gardstein and Levi, the dead assassin of Grove Street and owner of the "arsenal" in Gold Street, Stepney, resembled, by a coincidence, the elusive "Peter the Painter", and like the latter, was known for his skill with the brush.' Several days later, even more confusingly, it claimed there were two Fritz Svaars! In America, Pinkerton's Detective Agency publicly announced that they thought they could identify the Houndsditch murderers with three burglars who had committed a jewel robbery in Boston the previous March and subsequently jumped bail; fortunately for the harassed police this was quickly disproved with photographs.

The identification of both men, in fact, rested almost exclusively on Betsy Gershon's evidence to the Coroner's Inquest on 9 January 1911. She explained that she and her husband had come to England in 1905 but because of poor health he had gone back to Yalta in the Crimea eighteen months previously, where she occasionally sent him money. (Because of his wife's involvement in the 'siege', the Russian police subsequently searched his house and exiled him to another town.) She had met Joseph since her husband left, and he used to visit her once a week or once a fortnight. When he came on New Year's Day the first thing she noticed was that he had shaved off his moustache. Fritz was with him, but Joseph referred to him only as 'a pal'. When they came again the next night they refused to leave. They threatened her with their fists and made her take off her skirt and shoes to stop her going downstairs. She took a pillow and went to sleep in the stock room where there was a discarded sofa. About an hour later she heard Mrs Fleishmann knock on her door.

She described Joseph's peculiar limp, and her description of the man with him tallied with the official police description of Fritz Svaars. Dr Grant found on examination that body no. 1 had a spine more than an inch longer than that of body no. 2 and in every way was that of a bigger man. His right thigh-bone showed an old fracture well knitted, but which might have caused a limp in consequence of the shortening of the limb. It was safe to assume this was Joseph's body. From the position of the entrance and exit wounds in the head, the hole in the occipital bone behind the ear and the haemorrhage in the brain showing that the victim was alive when the wound was made, there was little doubt that he had been shot and had not committed suicide. From the fact that there was a considerable amount of rubbish under the body and that it had assumed a half-upright position among the accumulated rubbish, it was inferred by both Dr Grant and Station Officer Clark who found it that the body, although lying on the ground-floor back room when found, had fallen into that position from one of the upper rooms.

Body no. 2 was found by the doorway of the same room but without any rubbish under it, which suggested that Fritz had died where he was found lying. The body had been splashed with molten lead but had been protected to some extent by the debris which had fallen on top of it. Some clothing still remained; as far as Grant could judge it was the remains of two shirts (16½ collar) and two blue-serge waistcoats. The remains of male genital organs were quite visible but the other organs had been so destroyed by fire as to make any examination of them quite futile. The lower part of the face, including the mouth through which the tongue was protruding, the nose and parts of the orbits were present, and the signs unmistakably pointed to death by suffocation. The Coroner's jury brought in a verdict of justifiable homicide.

The bodies were enclosed in two plain elm coffins, one bearing the name Fritz Svaars and the other Joseph. They were taken to Ilford Cemetery and carried into the church with several other coffins. When the chaplain was told of their identity he expressed his strong disapproval of their bodies being brought into the church and said that it was an outrage to public decency that they should be buried in the same ground as two of the murdered policemen. The first part of the church service was read over their coffins, but a cemetery official directed that they should not be interred pending a decision of the cemetery authorities. The coffins were carried from the graveside and replaced on the hearse. Later the same day they were buried in unconsecrated ground without a religious service.

The 'siege' had created a sensation both at home and abroad. Foreign capitals reacted with humour, amazement, contempt and admiration. An American newspaper, wrongly reporting the death of Peter the Painter, said: 'It had been hoped, according to some ironical newspapers, that when he was run to earth an opportunity might have been given to the navy to share in the credit of the extermination of the Houndsditch murderers. The suggestion was that a torpedo boat destroyer should be anchored at the nearest point in the Thames and bombard the desperadoes' lair while 5000 policemen marshalled the London populace at a safe distance.'

In France there was nothing but admiration for British methods. There had been no 'hesitation, carping criticisms, vacillation, temporising' as would have happened in their own country. Most French newspapers believed that the two men, by attempting to stab in the back the country that had given them asylum, had swayed moderate opinion against them and perhaps dealt a deadly blow to international anarchism.

In Germany new restrictions were put on immigrants. The *Lokalanzeiger* sneered: 'As for us, a thousand policemen, troops, firemen, and machine-guns, would never be necessary to capture a criminal in Berlin. Our police would also think it their business to take the criminals alive. The action of the London police is comparable to the shooting of sparrows with cannon.'

Both at home and abroad, liberal journals hoped that the right of asylum would not be curtailed, while the anti-semitic press capitalised on the fact that the percentage of Jews in the revolutionary enterprises was high; it mocked the liberals for having praised the Russian terrorists as martyrs as long as they operated in Russia and condemned them as criminals as soon as they threatened the position of aliens in England. The Jewish newspapers blamed St Petersburg, and the Russians asked for international co-operation to stamp out anarchism.

At home there was heavy criticism of the police, and particularly of Churchill, for their handling of the affair. The police were blamed for not bringing out the men alive and there were dramatic suggestions that they should have climbed onto the roof and hurtled glass bowls of sulphurous acid down the chimney, or bored holes through the walls on both sides, at floor and ceiling level in each room, and fired through these until the men surrendered. An early newsreel of 'Mr Churchill directing the operations' was nightly received with unanimous boos and shouts of 'shoot him' from the gallery.

There was general astonishment at the poor quality of the weapons the police were armed with, and firearms manufacturers were invited by the Home Office to a basement shooting-gallery in Kennington to demonstrate new weapons. The gunsmith Robert Churchill was in charge of the tests. As well as police and Home Office officials, the Home Secretary was present. Before the gunsmith could begin, the Home Secretary, thinking he was the Mr Churchill being asked to start the trials, stepped forward eagerly and picked up a Mauser similar to the one he had carried in the cavalry charge at Omdurman and in the Boer War. A policeman obligingly shone his lamp along the barrel so that he could see the sights.

Neither the Home Office nor the City Corporation would accept any liability for the damage that had been done in Sidney Street. Churchill suggested that claims totalling more than £2000 should be referred for investigation to a board appointed by himself, consisting of representatives of the Metropolitan and City police and the Metropolitan police district. As far as he was aware there was no legal liability upon the police, or upon any public authority, to pay the claims, but it had always been the practice of the Metropolitan police to pay reasonable compensation, as an act of grace, to innocent by-standers whose property had been destroyed or damaged in efforts to make arrests. He suggested that, in the circumstances, this practice should be followed and any amount awarded paid in equal moiety by the Metropolitan police and the City Corporation. The City agreed on the understanding that they admitted no legal liability, and nominated the former Deputy Chairman of the Police Committee, Alpheus Morton, MP, as their representative. Churchill nominated Sir Henry Dalziel, MP, as the Home Office representative and W. J. Wilby of the Receiver's Office, Scotland Yard, as Secretary and Financial Adviser.

Most of the claims were wildly inflated. Charles Martin, the owner of the house, was bluntly told by the Committee that it had no intention of rebuilding it like Buckingham Palace. Nor would it compensate shopkeepers for lost profits and business, spoiled bread, advertising and brass bands, nor neighbours for miscarriages. Its only concern, it seemed, was for the former tenants who had had everything destroyed. Mrs Schiemann had died three weeks later, apparently from post-natal causes; her husband, left with four motherless children to support, could only find broken cups and plates in the ruins, and was compensated with £65. Old Mr Clements, whom he had carried out, was represented at the hearing by his grandchildren, who unwisely included in his claim nearly £12 for books he did not possess. They copied the titles from a bookseller's catalogue, and stupidly included the catalogue numbers and prices!

The Committee was even more disbelieving with the Fleishmanns' claims. Eyebrows were raised when Samuel Fleishmann honestly, if mistakenly, admitted that he had not paid income tax for the past eleven years. His equally frank admission that nothing had been insured placed the Committee in a quandary; it was not sure whether to let him suffer for his negligence or compensate him out of pity. As a businessman he was a failure and for some years had obviously been living on capital. Losing his stock and machines had put him out of business. His claim for more than £900 was nearly half the total amount claimed. Not unnaturally the Committee scrutinised each item in great detail. It was highly sceptical of the silver spoons, and of the beaver coats, diamond rings, gold chain, and the evening dress-suit the landlord claimed he wore. It gave him just over a quarter of what he asked for.

The only tenant the Committee refused to compensate was Mrs Gershon. No charge had been brought against her and she was released, but few people were willing to help her. The Committee was openly hostile and crudely implied that she had been Joseph's mistress or worse.

On 20 January 1911 the City Police Commissioner asked the General Purposes Committee of Aldermen to give him the money to pay the informer who had led them to the wanted men. He was not mentioned by name. If Charles Perelman had expected the full £500, he was disappointed. The full sum was for three people – Fritz Svaars, Peter the Painter and the unnamed woman. Since he had led them only to one he was only entitled to a third. He was paid £166 13s 4d.

Joseph was worth nothing.

IX

The Judas Window

RAIN gusted across the Guildhall yard as the committal proceedings of the Houndsditch murders began. Gas flares were burning brightly in the eighteenth-century court-house on the left of the yard, even though it was late morning, as the horse-drawn prison-van rolled through the line of policemen surrounding the square and the armed policeman, who had been sitting by the driver, climbed stiffly to the ground. Under their waterlogged capes every policeman was carrying a revolver.

Sara Trassjonsky was gripped by the arms and hurried into court between a detective and a prison matron. Since her arrest she had broken down completely. The lingering hours of watching Gardstein die, her abandonment by everyone, including Luba, the hours of waiting by the body for the police to come and arrest her, and her present plight, had nudged her over the edge into hopeless insanity. There were occasional patches of lucidity, but these were getting fewer and fewer and would shortly disappear altogether. Since she was thirteen years old her life had been nothing more than 'agony, hunger, cold, misery and illness'. There had hardly been a day when she was free from the pains in her head and crippled back. Her home life had been brutalised by her father's shoutings, and the occasional beating-up of her mother, when the children huddled in a corner of the room, not daring to go out; afterwards her mother, to relieve her own misery, would give them a punch or smack.

In the notes she had scribbled in the police station after her arrest, and which were taken by the police for possible clues, she had described how Gardstein's body, like Banquo's ghost, had loomed suddenly before her eyes; how she could hear voices shouting at her that she had killed him; then there was the relief when she thought that she had betrayed everyone and could run free in the streets because there was nobody left to kill her; and finally, a recurring theme, that it was for her mother's sins she was suffering.

Her letters, written in moments of lucidity, as well as the other prisoners' letters, were handed to the police for translation in the hope of yielding possible clues. Those in Russian were translated by the Russian Consulate, who were thus in a position to pass to the Tsarist police not only information on the prisoners themselves but also the whereabouts of their friends and families and other possible dissidents. The prisoners' most frequent demands were for books and linen. Jacob Peters asked for books by Gorky and Zola, and Luba Milstein, in the martyr's role she had created for herself, *De Profundis*.

Jacob Peters, after an initial nervousness, was indifferent, genuinely so, as to what happened to him. His strength was his indifference to death. As the son of a Latvian farm-labourer he had experienced all the burdens of degrading forced labour. His schooling had lasted only a few winters; at the age of eight he was tending cattle, and at fourteen he had become a farm-labourer like his father. In 1904, when he was eighteen, he had left the farm and moved to Riga where he joined the illegal Latvian Social Democrats Labourers Party. During the war with Japan Peters founded a party cell in the Libau ship-building yard and openly agitated among the sailors of the Baltic Fleet. He led a strike in the shipbuilding yard, but in the terror which swiftly followed the 1905 uprising he was flung into prison on a fake attempted-murder charge. Not realising his importance, or the part he had played in the uprising, his captors had limited his torture to beatings-up and ripping out his fingernails. Later Peters recalled how they had tortured a fellow prisoner – who may well have been tortured with him –

by not only ripping out his fingernails, but also perforating his eardrums and tearing off his genitals.

Peters was detained for nearly two years. In the autumn of 1907 he and the other prisoners went on hunger strike and demanded to be manacled whenever they were taken out of the prison, as batches of prisoners that had formerly gone out had always been shot for allegedly escaping.

He had been released in 1909 and fled to England before the full extent of his complicity in the uprising was known. Peters joined several left-wing groups to improve his 'theoretical and political education', and studied English which he apparently spoke with a Cockney accent acquired in the sweat shop where he worked as a tailor's presser. Unquestionably his share of the expropriation, if it had succeeded, would have gone to Lenin and the Bolsheviks. He had no intention of shouldering responsibility when the police and Press were blaming Fritz and Peter the Painter for the murders, and there was a possibility of his wriggling out. His first words when he was arrested had been, 'It is nothing to do with me. I can't help what my cousin Fritz has done.' Yet even he must have wondered how he was going to shake the evidence of the eyewitness who had seen him and Dubof with guns in their hands dragging Gardstein out of Exchange Buildings.

Dubof had been arrested on the same day as Peters. By an incredible coincidence he had been recognised in the prison hospital by another prisoner, John Hayes, who was completely unknown to him but who had seen him in Exchange Buildings on the day of the robbery, not once but three times. Hayes had been a policeman for twelve years, before being dismissed and sentenced to a month's hard labour for theft; several minor convictions had followed and he was on release when he saw Dubof. He hadn't been surprised at the close scrutiny Dubof had given him as the years in the force had left their mark and he was used to being mistaken for a detective. When he saw Dubof in the prison hospital he immediately recognised him again and suspected at once that he might be connected with the murders. He slipped him a newspaper with Gardstein's picture on the front page to see how he reacted. Dubof went deadly pale and repeatedly kissed the photograph before folding it up and putting it under his pillow.

Hayes immediately told the prison governor and the police. His story was checked and found to be true. In his statement he described a woman who had been standing with Dubof in Exchange Buildings, but omitted to mention another man who had been standing only a few feet away. On 15/16 February 1911 he saw this man exercising in the prison yard. Hayes only knew him as B1-26, the prison governor as John Rosen alias 'the Barber'.

Rosen's whereabouts hadn't been known until mid-January. Inspector Wensley had missed him by ten minutes when he visited Nina Vassilleva two days after the murders, and after that he had disappeared. Tomacoff knew him only by his nickname. The trail might have ended there except that Rosen became careless and told Rose Campbell, a girl he had been courting for eight months, that he was involved with the group. She in turn confided in her mother, who told her son-in-law Edward Humphreys, who went to the police. Humphreys said that on Christmas Eve Rosen had taken Rose Campbell to a house off the Commercial Road and introduced her to a man he said was Peter the Painter, a friend of his and the man wanted by the police. Rosen had also told her that he was a member of the gang and that if anyone had fallen out on the night of the murders he would have taken his place. He said that he knew about the Tottenham Outrage, although he didn't go into details, and that a reward had been offered by the Russian Government for the arrest of Gardstein for a similar outrage in Russia. Mr Humphreys ended by saying that in October Rosen had taken Rose Campbell to his room where he had assaulted and seduced her. The police had not started proceedings against him as the girl had gone to his room of her own free will.

Rose Campbell promptly denied the whole story when she was questioned and, on 31 January 1911, married her alleged seducer. Her mother would only go as far as saying that, as

Rosen was a foreigner, she thought he might be connected with the gang. She identified a photograph of Gardstein as a man she had once seen with her son-in-law. On 2 February Rosen was arrested at the barber's shop where he worked. His first words were, 'I know you have come to arrest me.'

For three days he denied everything. Then, on Sunday morning, 5 February, he called through the Judas window in his cell door and asked Police Constable Woodward, 'What will they do with me, if I know something and don't tell them?' Woodward answered, 'Do you know anything about this affair?' Rosen nodded. 'I could show you where a man and a woman live, or were living, who are concerned in it, but I don't know if they have moved since I have been here.' His cell was unlocked and he was taken to the headquarters in Old Jewry to make a statement.

Rosen had arrived in England from Riga in January 1909 and had gone to live in a sailors' lodging-house at No. 1 High Street, Poplar, run by a carpenter called Stroch; according to police information, Stroch was an anarchist and a police spy, allegedly on the run from Russia for murder; he was also supposed to arrange robberies and then inform the police. Rosen not only lived but worked on the premises in a small barber's-shop. After he had been there about three or four months he struck up a casual acquaintance with Bifsteks, who came to live there, and through him he was introduced to the Perelmans and the rest of the group at the lodging-house in Great Garden Street. He admitted going to Grove Street on the day of the murders but said that he had spent the evening with Hoffman at the pictures, and later in his room, before going home. Next day, when he had heard of the murders, he had gone back and asked Hoffman what had happened. Hoffman had told him briefly what he knew, how Fritz, Joseph, Peter and Luba had come to his room and how he wouldn't let them stay. Apart from that he knew nothing. Rosen had visited him twice more. The third time he went to 36 Lindley Street Hoffman had fled.

Nina Vassilleva was already being watched, but the whereabouts of Hoffman's lodgings opened up a completely new line of enquiry. Only Luba Milstein could have given them his address, but since her arrest she had been detained in the prison hospital and would say nothing, possibly on her solicitor's advice. When questioned by the police Hoffman's landlord said that he had ordered him out of the house the day after the 'siege'; the tenant on the next floor had complained that he could not sleep because Hoffman paced about the room and continually opened and shut the windows. He had left the same night at about 10 p.m. but nine or ten days later a woman had brought the landlord a note from Hoffman asking for some clothes he had left behind and for any letters to be forwarded to Mrs Janson, 114 Cannon Street. The woman said that Hoffman was afraid to go out, and she herself was afraid that she would suffer through him.

Mrs Janson's husband, Theodore, had been helping the police as an informer since 23 December at least, which was when he made his first statement, but it was now clear that he was playing a double game. He was twenty-nine years old and had emigrated from Riga with his wife and children in 1905; he earned his living as a bicycle-maker. In his first statement he had given the police a false name, and an accommodation address used by Fritz in Stepney. Subsequently he had related how he had met Hoffman on Christmas Day and asked him if Peters, Dubof and Federoff, who had been arrested, were the men involved. Hoffman had laughed and said, 'No, there were nine men in the plot, none of them are yet arrested. It's a pity the man is dead [meaning Gardstein], he was the ablest of the lot and leader of the gang. He also managed it that some members of the gang didn't know the others.' Janson had said, at the time, that he didn't know Hoffman's address, but this now seemed unlikely. He had also said that he knew Gardstein lived in Stepney and would try to find out his address, but to do that he needed money. Next day, at the same time that Gardstein's landlord recognised the photograph on the reward poster and went to Arbour Square police station, Janson called back and said that Hoffman had sent a message asking him to go to 44 Gold Street to collect from the landlady three leather

trunks belonging to Gardstein. He was too late. The Stepney
Bomb Factory, as it was called by the newspapers, had already
been found.

Now that they knew Janson was playing a double game the
police made their preparations accordingly. They raided Janson's
house at 2.15 in the morning of 8 February. There were to be
no more 'sieges'. Armed police surrounded the house and got
the other tenants out, including Janson and his family, without
waking the wanted man. Hoffman was still asleep when he was
yanked to his feet and half dragged, half carried to the shop
next door. He tried to bluff his way out with the help of
Janson who said that he wasn't the man referred to in his statement. His protests were ignored. A jacket which Janson had
lent him, and which was in the room where he was sleeping,
had in one of the pockets a passport in the name of Trohimtchick, which was the alias Fritz had used at Newcastle Place;
but Hoffman denied that the jacket belonged to him. In the
other jacket were five letters and the return half of a ticket to
Antwerp. From these the police were able to piece together his
movements over the past month. He had gone back to Riga,
but on 27 January the Tsarist police had surrounded the house
where he was staying and he had only just managed to escape
back to England via Antwerp. He had been living since then
with the Jansons. Letters for him had been addressed to Mrs
Janson and he had identified which were his by the handwriting.
The only one of the group he would admit he knew was Fritz,
and then only by his Christian name; the others were just faces
he had seen at clubs and concerts.

A few hours earlier the net had also closed around Nina
Vassilleva. She had been watched for nearly eight weeks and
followed wherever she went. Ironically, she was arrested while
walking through Sidney Street. Incredibly, although she had
expected her arrest at any time, the detectives found in her room
not only newspaper cuttings on the murders but the blue three-
quarter-length coat she had been wearing on the night of the
murders, and which still had large patches of dried blood on
the front (see above, page 96). On 14 February she and Rosen

were formally charged in front of the magistrates with conspiracy to rob, and next day Hoffman was charged with the
same offence.

From the prisoners' point of view the most disastrous day of
the magistrates'-court hearing so far was Rosen's committal,
since the police read out not only his original statement
denying everything but the subsequent statements as well
betraying Nina Vassilleva and Hoffman. The latter was
appalled that he should have said so much. Rosen wanted to
explain his motives but although he, Hoffman and Dubof were
on the same landing in Brixton Gaol, they had no way of
communicating until Rosen struck up a conversation with a
prisoner called Arthur Weeks, a farm-labourer awaiting trial
for the carnal knowledge of his nine-year-old stepdaughter. He
had already served one sentence for killing sheep and had other
convictions for drunkenness and poaching.

Either on Friday, 17 or Saturday, 18 February he was working outside cell B1-23 when Rosen called him, 'What are you
in for?'

'Carnal knowledge,' Weeks growled.

Rosen's English was not good enough. 'Don't understand,'
he said.

'What are you in for?' Weeks asked.

'Conspiracy,' Rosen said, and pushed his card through the
door.

Weeks studied it for a moment. 'You are charged with breaking into somebody's shop.'

Rosen nodded his head. 'How do you think I shall get on?
Two witnesses say I was carrying a bag twice.' (He had been
identified as carrying a green bag out of Exchange Buildings
on two occasions.)

'Did you carry a bag?' Weeks asked.

'Yes.'

'Did they see you?'

'The witnesses say they did.'

'You will get eighteen months.' Weeks sniffed and walked
away.

Later the same afternoon he was cleaning cell tins on the landing when Rosen pushed through the grate part of an envelope with a message scrawled on it in a foreign language. 'You, 27,' he said. Weeks took it to Dubof in cell B1-27. About an hour and a half later he was sorting Bibles and prayerbooks when Dubof gave him a message scrawled on lavatory paper to take back.

Weeks was not on the landing again until Monday morning at 7.30 when he gave the prisoners their tea. When he was outside B1-4 Hoffman pushed three pieces of lavatory paper through the grate and asked him to give them to Dubof. Instead Weeks took them to his cell, but when he discovered that he couldn't read them he folded them up again and passed them to the warder. He did the same thing with a message Dubof threw to him that afternoon to give to Hoffman. Both were translated by the police.

Hoffman thought that the Barber was trying to save his own neck at the expense of the others. His own view was that there was no point in confessing as the police were looking for twenty-eight people – they believed this to be the size of the group – and wouldn't call off the hunt for the others. The Prison Governor questioned him about the note but Hoffman said it was only a friendly message and denied knowing Dubof before his arrest. He persisted in his denial even when the Governor produced Dubof's note suggesting that they should say that they had only known one another since March or April 1910, when Dubof was living at Wellesley Street. From April to September, the note continued, Dubof had been in Switzerland but they had kept in touch and afterwards met intermittently when they were both looking for jobs. They had gone to Grove Street on 16 December to discuss the decorations for the Lettish concert. Dubof was worried because he had told his lawyer that he had gone to Hoffman's lodgings on 18 December, but if possible he didn't want this mentioned although he had been seen there on that occasion by Hoffman's landlord and landlady; if they didn't mention this in their evidence neither would he. Since then, they were to say, they hadn't met. Dubof wasn't sure whether it was wise to make a confession or not; he would ask his lawyer if it meant a lighter sentence. Until then he advised against it. There was no point in making trouble unnecessarily. It was best to wait and see. They must continue to stress that they were just ordinary working men and casual acquaintances.

About the same time Weeks, having handed their notes to the warder, was in the exercise yard walking along two yards behind Jacob Peters.

'How are you getting on with your affair?' he muttered.

Peters turned his head and looked over his left shoulder. 'I shall get about five or six years,' he said in broken English.

For a man standing in the shadow of the gallows this seemed unduly optimistic.

X

Red Circles in Court

THE most telling point in the defendants' favour, although they didn't realise it at the time, was that the arrests were made over a period of nearly two months – from the time of the first hearing on 21 December 1910, when Trassjonsky and Milstein were brought before the Guildhall court, to 15 February when the last prisoner, Hoffman, was charged.* Evidence was consequently introduced in a piece-meal fashion, and points vital to the prosecution's case were lost in the increasing complexity of evidence.

On 23 January 1911 Mr Bodkin opened the case for the Crown against the five who were then in custody – Peters, Dubof, Federoff, Milstein and Trassjonsky. None of them were supposed to have more than a smattering of English, but it quickly became apparent from their gestures that they were having little difficulty in following the evidence. He began by saying that the three men were implicated in the murder of the three policemen, that the two women were accessories after the fact, and that all five were concerned in the attempted burglary of Harris's shop.

'It was an enterprise which could not be entered upon and carried out in a few hours, required some long time to get into proper working order, and therefore we hear that as early as

* The committal proceedings were actually spread over four months. See below, page 152.

21 November there were enquiries for a house in Exchange Buildings. . . .'

He told the court that Joe Levi, who had rented No. 11, had never been traced but later in the hearing the police learned from Luba Milstein that Joe Levi was, beyond question, Max Smoller (see above, page 47).

The prosecution's two principal witnesses were Isaac Levy and George Richardson, a jeweller's assistant in Houndsditch, who was also friendly with the boy Solomon Abrahams, who on several occasions had pointed out the new tenants of 9 and 11 Exchange Buildings to him when he had seen them in the street. Consequently Richardson had recognised Gardstein at once when the latter had tried to draw him into conversation late one evening and get him to discuss the better kinds of jewellers' shops in Houndsditch, mentioning Harris's by name. On another occasion he had seen Gardstein drinking in the Three Nuns in Aldgate with Federoff, Peters and Dubof.

Other prosecution witnesses had come forward with equally damning evidence 'So that not only at the Jubilee Street Club, but at 59 Grove Street, in the public house, the Three Nuns, and in the neighbourhood of Cutler Street and at this very house No. 11 Exchange Buildings, there will be evidence to these prisoners, Federoff, Peters, and Dubof, being in direct association with Fritz and "Peter the Painter".'

Mr Bodkin blundered badly from the beginning. His first and greatest mistake was when he deduced that, since Gardstein was the man who opened the door to Bentley, it was Gardstein also who started the shooting.

Gardstein was the man who came in flinging open that back door and shot Bentley at his right front; there were also other shots from the man on the stairs. . . . Several shots were fired at Bentley by the man Gardstein from the back, he advanced to the front door of the house, of that there is no doubt, for we have the hand, according to the evidence of Strongman, protruding through the door of No. 11, so as to sweep the place, firing at Woodhams, Bryant and Martin. That man Gardstein advanced further, for you will remember in the evidence of Strongman he said he came out and fired at him and Sergeant Tucker while they were in the roadway of Exchange Buildings.

The later finding of the Dreyse pistol which had fatally wounded the three policemen, with Gardstein's body, apparently confirmed this interpretation as the correct one.

Unfortunately it wasn't. It was a blunder of colossal proportions. Only two alternatives had been open to Gardstein after he partly closed the door on Bentley. Either he could go up the stairs behind him or through the ground-floor room, which didn't have a connecting door with the hall, into the yard. From where he was standing outside, Constable Martin had had a clear view through the partly open street-door into the brightly lit room and must have seen Gardstein if he had crossed his line of vision. As he didn't Gardstein must have gone upstairs. He was the man standing at the top of the stairs with his face in darkness when Bentley pushed open the door a few seconds later.

The next point to be borne in mind is the survivors' description of the man who, in fact, did come in from the backyard. Only two policemen saw him – Sergeant Bryant, who had been standing in the doorway with Bentley, and Constable Strongman who had dragged the dying Tucker out of the firing.

Bryant told the court that just before the shooting started Bentley had been speaking to the man on the stairs. As Bentley had moved further into the room Bryant had stepped into the passage after him.

Immediately I saw a man coming from the back door of the room between Bentley and the table. On 6 January I went to the City of London Mortuary and there saw a dead body and I recognised the man. I noticed he had a pistol in his hand, and at once commenced to fire towards Bentley's right shoulder. He was just in the room. The shots were fired very rapidly. I distinctly heard 3 or 4. I at once put up my hands and I felt my left hand fall and I fell out on to the footway. Immediately the man commenced to fire Bentley staggered back against the door post of the opening into the room. The appearance of the pistol struck me as being a long one. I think I should know a similar one again if I saw it. Only one barrel, and it seemed to me to be a black one. I next remember getting up and staggered along by the wall for a few yards until I recovered myself. I was going away from Cutler Street. I must have been dazed as I have a very faint recollection of what happened then.

Bryant's positive identification of Gardstein as Bentley's attacker is certainly open to question. 'Immediately' twice, and 'rapidly', stress the speed at which the shootings began. Bentley is staggering backwards towards Bryant as the bullets tear into his throat and shoulder. At the same time Bryant himself is under fire from the man on the stairs and is stumbling into the street with bullets in his arm and chest. At best, Bryant could only have had a snap impression of what was happening. His positive identification of Gardstein three weeks later is in line with the, by then, official version of the incident.

Still more erroneous is his evidence that the pistol being fired had a long black barrel, suggesting a Mauser, two of which had been found in Sidney Street. If, in fact, the man who came through the door was carrying a Mauser, it couldn't have been his shots which hit Bentley, because the post mortem showed that the only bullets which hit the sergeant and fatally wounded Tucker and Choat had been fired from the same Dreyse, a much smaller pistol. (Choat had also been shot with a Mauser but the shots that killed him had been fired from the Dreyse.)

The same gun also killed Sergeant Tucker. Constable Strongman again identified Gardstein as the attacker, although his original statement, which includes a description of the killer, shows that it could not have been. Worse still, Strongman only identified Gardstein from a photograph and did not even see the body. In his statement Strongman wrote:

The door was opened by some person whom I did not see. P.S. Bentley appeared to have a conversation with the person, and the door was then partly closed, shortly afterwards P.S. Bentley pushed the door open and entered, about a minute later I heard several shots and saw P.S. Bentley fall from the doorway across the step. Other shots followed in quick succession and a hand holding a revolver, firing rapidly, protruded from the doorway of No. 11 Exchange Buildings and was pointed at P.C. Woodhams who I saw fall forward into the carriageway. That hand was followed by a man age about 30, height 5' 6" or 7", pale thin face, dark curly hair, and dark moustache, dress dark jacket suit, no hat, who pointed the revolver in the direction of P.S. Tucker and myself, firing rapidly. P.S. Tucker and I stepped back a few yards when the P.S. staggered and turned round. I caught him by the right arm, and we walked towards Cutler Street. I looked over my left shoulder and saw the man fire two more shots in our direction, then he turned and went back in the direction of No. 11 Exchange Buildings. The whole of the shooting appeared to be over in ten seconds.

In court he expanded on some details. He was standing with Sergeant Tucker when

I heard 3 or 4 shots fired, and we made a step towards the door, when I saw a hand holding a pistol protrude from the street doorway of No. 11, firing rapidly, pointing towards P.C. Woodhams, who was opposite No. 11 Exchange Buildings. I saw P.C. Woodhams fall towards the carriageway; this man came out of the doorway still holding the pistol and pointed it towards Sergeant Tucker and myself, firing rapidly all the time. We stepped back, Sergeant Tucker turned round and staggered. Seeing he was wounded I put my arm round his and led him towards Cutler Street. I looked over my left shoulder and saw the man fire two more shots in our direction, and I could also see the flashes coming from the doorway of No. 11. He turned and went back in the direction of No. 11. . . . I could only see the barrel as he came under the lamp and it looked a long thin one. The shooting only lasted about 10 seconds and may have been less.

Only Strongman was able to describe the killer in detail. The only doubtful evidence in his two statements is that relating to the pistol which he suggests, but does not positively identify, as a 'long thin one'; suggesting again a Mauser. Possibly he did

see a Mauser barrel protruding from the doorway because it
was from the doorway that he saw Constable Woodhams shot
and a Mauser bullet was later extracted from Woodham's leg.
However, the man who stepped into the street and, walking
towards him and Tucker, shot the sergeant twice – once in the
hip and once in the heart – was firing the same Dreyse pistol
that had been used moments before to kill Bentley. Ballistics
evidence showed it to be the same one. Apart from his curly
hair the most important thing Strongman noticed about him
was his jacket suit.

At this point in his statement, the shootings were reaching
their climax. Bentley and Tucker were dying, Strongman was
dragging the latter out of the firing, Martin was hiding, Bryant
and Woodhams were wounded and unconscious, one propped
up against a house and the other lying in the roadway, and
Piper and Smoothey were running from Houndsditch to the
cul-de-sac. From this it is reasonable to infer that when the
killer of Bentley and Tucker turned, as Strongman said he did,
he did so because he had heard or seen Gardstein grappling
with Constable Choat.

Choat's wounds included four in the left leg, thigh, calf and
foot. One bullet was extracted from the leg and was identified as
having been fired from a Mauser or Borchardt auto-pistol of .30
calibre; another fragment in the leg also came from a Mauser.
Choat was a big man, 6 feet 4 inches, and Gardstein a mere
5 feet 8 inches. The brief struggle between them was obviously
an unequal one except that Gardstein was armed and Choat
was not. There were burn marks on Choat's uniform where the
pistol had flowered against the cloth, and it is not too fanciful to
suggest that, when Choat ran towards Gardstein and caught
him, he gripped him by the wrist which was holding the Mauser.
Gardstein, trying to break free, pulled the trigger four times as
Choat pushed his hand down and away to deflect the shots.
Although the shots missed his vital organs, Choat could not stop
them hitting him in the leg, thigh, calf and foot.

As Choat's leg buckled beneath him, he was shot twice, with
two carefully placed shots in the back, from the same Dreyse

that had already killed Bentley and Tucker. He fell backwards dragging Gardstein with him, and as they fell Gardstein was accidentally shot in the back by Max Smoller.

Now the importance of Strongman's evidence becomes obvious. Under the street light he had noticed not only the curly hair of the man firing the Dreyse but that he was wearing a jacket suit. *It could not have been Gardstein firing the Dreyse because he was wearing an overcoat when he was shot. It was found with the bullet hole in the back, just under the bloodstained left shoulder, and matching the wound in his body.* Clearly it was impossible for Gardstein to have been grappling with a man who was not only bigger but nearly a foot taller than himself, to have fired four shots into his leg with a Mauser pistol which the policeman was trying to take away, and in the same instant that he himself was shot in the back to have got behind his opponent who was dragging him to the ground and killed him with a completely different gun!

Who was firing the Dreyse, then? Who was the man who killed Bentley, Tucker and Choat? It could not have been Max because he shot Gardstein with a Browning. Besides he was clean-shaven, and whoever was firing the Dreyse was similar enough in appearance to Gardstein to be mistaken for him by both Bryant and Strongman – they had described him as 'age about 30, height 5′ 6″ or 7″, pale thin face, dark curly hair and dark moustache . . .'. This only leaves Jacob Peters and Yourka Dubof. Both were of similar height and build to Gardstein – there was only 1½ inches difference between all three – and both had moustaches. But, as can be seen from the photographs taken after their arrest (see plates), only Peters had the dark curly hair and moustache to be mistaken for Gardstein. Dubof's light-coloured moustache barely shows.

Jacob Peters was the killer of Bentley, Tucker and Choat. And he was in custody. But the whole of the prosecution's case rested on the mistaken assumption that it was Gardstein who killed Tucker, Bentley and Choat. Though Mr Bodkin realised that there were doubts about the firearms the police had described, he glossed over their statements. He said that one could well understand that these officers – he thought Bryant was one – were wrong in saying that the man who was firing at Bentley had a 'long thin barrel pistol'. 'I hope I may never have to observe the kind of pistol a person is firing at me.' Any further doubts as to who really did the shooting were stifled completely when he came to describe the finding of Gardstein's body.

Now Gardstein – under his pillow at 59 Grove Street was found exhibit No. 2, which was a Dreyse pistol. A pistol with a magazine, which on examination had been recently fired. It is difficult to say – for any expert to say – when it had been recently fired. It was a pistol rifled in four grooves, and Mr Goodwin, a gentleman who has kindly examined this pistol . . . has fired some shots from that pistol into sawdust.

The cartridges which can be fired from that pistol are quite common cartridges which are standardised and are used for various automatic pistols, but the peculiarity of this Dreyse pistol is that it has four grooves. It appears that six bullets – two from Tucker's body, two from Bentley's body and two from Choat's body – were fired from the Dreyse pistol as they all have four groove marks upon them. . . . It is clear that Gardstein was the man who fired, and under his pillow a Dreyse pistol was found, and it seems quite proper to assume that he it was who used the Dreyse pistol. The only one to hit Bentley was Gardstein, and Bentley's bullets were from a Dreyse pistol.

Now even a cursory examination of the basic statements would have shown that the Dreyse was most emphatically not found under the pillow and, by inference, within easy reach of Gardstein's hand to defend himself. The officer who had found the Dreyse when the room was searched was Detective Sergeant Leeson who had subsequently been wounded in the opening shots of the 'Siege'. Because of his lung wound he had been promoted and pensioned off with the higher pension. In his official report he wrote, 'Between the mattress and the palliasse I found one magazine pistol containing seven cartridges, two magazines (one containing seven and one containing six cartridges).' Inspector Thompson, who searched the room with him, confirmed this: 'Between the mattress and the palliasse at the head of the bed was also found a revolver loaded with seven cartridges, also two clips, one containing seven and the other six cartridges.' Ernest Goodwin, the prosecution's ballistics expert, was equally specific. 'The cartridges in the Dreyse pistol No. 7065, found between the mattress and palliasse of the bed on the first floor at Grove Street, E., those in the two clips found in the same place, and in Gardstein's clothing are 7.65 Belgian cartridges of F.N. manufacture.'

Now it has been wrongly assumed from Mr Bodkin's statement that the pistol was under the pillow for Gardstein to defend himself and to resist arrest. In support of this theory it has been alleged that a cap containing a quantity of ammunition was placed by the bed within easy reach of his hand. Certainly there was a cap with ammunition by the bed but none of it could be fired from the Dreyse! According to the ballistics expert the cap held 'six .297/230 short cartridges for Morris tubes and small rook rifles, six .30 Mauser pistol cartridges and seventeen 7.9 mm Mauser rifle cartridges of Hirtenberger [Austrian] 1904 manufacture'. According to Luba Milstein's evidence the cap was not there when Fritz, Joseph, Peter and Max left. Since she didn't put it there and Gardstein couldn't, it could only have been put there by Sara Trassjonsky when she was gathering up evidence to destroy. The ammunition was put in the cap for convenience as she bustled about the room and was never meant to be fired; it was meant to be thrown away.

If, in fact, Gardstein had owned the Dreyse, it is reasonable to suppose that some ammunition for this weapon would have been found in his lodgings, which were described as an arsenal as well as a bomb factory. None was found. The only ammunition 'consisted of . . . 308 .30 Mauser cartridges, some of D.W.M. [German] manufacture, and the other with plain heads; also 26 Hirtenberger 7.9 mm Mauser rifle cartridges'. It is inconceivable, surely, that a man would have over 300 rounds of ammunition for a Mauser pistol which he didn't possess, and none for the Dreyse he is supposed to have used!

All the evidence suggests that the Mauser pistol which Gardstein was using was handed over to, or taken by, Joseph, and was one of the burnt-out Mausers found in Sidney Street. Goodwin thought that the Browning that was also found there might have fired the bullet into Gardstein's back. Owing to the fire damage he was unable to remove the barrel and could only take a short sulphur-cast of the part of the barrel next to the chamber. The cast showed that the barrel was five-grooved and might also have fired the bullet that was found in No. 2 Exchange Buildings by Miss Parker. Nothing much could be gleaned from the Mausers. The cartridges had exploded from the heat of the fire and the leaden cores had melted and flowed away.

Having handed over his own gun to Joseph, why should Gardstein have a cap filled with ammunition he couldn't use placed by his bed and, when he was powerless to move, have a Dreyse he couldn't use thrust between the mattress and the palliasse where he couldn't possibly reach it, instead of under the pillow if, in fact, he had intended to resist arrest?

Inevitably the conclusion is that he didn't know the Dreyse was there. He thought that by getting rid of his Mauser he had rid himself of at least one major piece of incriminating evidence. His bullet wound he would try to explain away as the result of a shooting accident, as he in fact did to Dr Scanlon. What he didn't realise was that, thrust between the mattress and the palliasse on which he was lying in a state of shock, too ill and too weak to move, was the one piece of evidence which could hang him. If this interpretation is correct, the Dreyse could only have been put there by Peters. But, according to Mr Bodkin, Gardstein had been taken to Grove Street by Fritz Svaars and Peter the Painter, and not by Peters, who was last seen with Dubof and Vassilleva dragging the dying man out of Exchange Buildings.

Again Mr Bodkin didn't try to explain the discrepancy. He described how Isaac Levy had seen Peters and Dubof carrying Gardstein, and how they had threatened him and told him not to follow; how the workmen had seen them in Harrow Alley and Bell Lane the same group, doubtless, of four men and the middle man supported by one on either side of him, and there at that point the group is lost sight of but we get from the statements of Luba Milstein and Trassjonsky that at 59 Grove Street several men came in very shortly after midnight, and it was, of course – but it is obvious – that Gardstein was practically carried in. How did they get in? Fritz had a key. It is quite, but I do not think it is in evidence, possible that 'Peter the Painter' had a key. He was familiar with that house for he lived there for some time, and up that staircase, which is of a narrow and most awkward description, that man Gardstein was taken by someone entirely familiar with the ways of that house and staircase. That several persons were there is clear from the statements of Milstein and Trassjonsky, for they said they heard footsteps and the voices of several men.

But how could Mr Bodkin say that Fritz and Peter had carried Gardstein into the house when Luba and Sara had heard only footsteps? This is clear from Luba's final cross-examination:

'To the police when you gave yourself up you said, "I heard the steps of two or three persons, I could not see who they were." '

'Yes.'

'That was not true was it?'

'It was true.'

'"I could not see who they were." Is that true?'

'I did not see them when they came in, I saw them afterwards.'

'You went on to say to the police, "We heard someone go downstairs, I believe two men, I did not see them."'

'I stated that in my first statement, I stated differently in the second.'

'That was not true to say you did not see them?'

'No.'

'How many men in all did you see?'

'Three.'

'Might there have been others there?'

'I do not know.'

But Luba only changed her evidence because the prosecution

were insisting that the men she had seen go out were the same men who had brought the dying Gardstein to the house, although all along she had denied that they were. Besides, Fritz himself, in his last letter, had said quite plainly that two men had brought Gardstein to his rooms where he had been all evening. Not surprisingly, as by this time she had been made a witness for the defence, Luba agreed to this interpretation of the facts as it increased the other prisoners' chances of acquittal. It also made her evidence that Fritz had told her he had carried Gardstein through the streets like a baby much more believable. The dead man had to become a scapegoat if the others were to escape the gallows.

But rarely in any murder trial, could the prosecution have contributed so much to the destruction of its own case.

The committal proceedings were spread over *four months*, from December to March, and comprised twenty-four separate hearings. Luba Milstein's counsel soon protested against the succession of remands which were made without a case ever being opened against her. He pointed out that she had voluntarily surrendered herself to the police and since she had been in custody they had been unable to show that she was in any way connected with the crime. At the opening of the proceedings of 21 February Mr Bodkin told the court that on the evidence which had so far been given there was insufficient evidence for the prosecution to justify her further detention on the charges of accessory to murder and conspiracy. On the advice of her solicitors she had already made a statement supplemental to the evidence that was already before the court and he asked that she should be discharged. Through the interpreter Luba Milstein was told that she was free to go.

She turned at once – she had been sitting between Trassjon-sky and Vassilleva – and without a look at the other prisoners she pushed past Nina and stumbled up the stairs to the back of the court, her dull heavy face lit up by a smile. Her brother took her outside at once, but before she reached the outer doors she broke into a fit of hysterical sobbing. Outside she leaned against the wall of the court and continued sobbing until her brother calmed her down and, when she was more composed, led her away.

The previous week, on 15 February, Karl Hoffman had been brought before the court for the first time charged with conspiracy to break and enter. He was more smartly dressed than any of the other prisoners; over a lounge suit he wore a dark overcoat with a velvet collar. In the dock he engaged in an animated conversation with Dubof and Rosen. Possibly this hurried exchange was to flush out their smuggled prison-notes to each other. This sudden intimacy surprised the court when Hoffman's statement, with his corrections, was read out to them. Not only did he deny knowing Rosen and Dubof with whom he was having an animated conversation, but also Gardstein, Joseph, Peter the Painter, Federoff, Peters, Trassjonsky, Smoller and Vassilleva! In custody he had been shown photographs of Gardstein, Rosen, Federoff and Peter the Painter and had recognised them as men he had seen; he identified Jacob Peters, also from a photograph, as someone he had seen at Lettish concerts. The only people he would admit knowing were Luba Milstein and Fritz, who, he said, had introduced her as his wife. On 16 December he had gone to bed at midnight and nobody had visited his room. He had heard about the murders the next morning and later heard from a Russian acquaintance that Fritz – he did not know his name was Svaars – was concerned in the murders. Not unnaturally he was appalled at just how much Rosen had given away and the full extent of his revelations as to what had really happened. He frankly disbelieved him when he said he had done this to help them, and was convinced that the Barber wanted to 'come out with a whole skin' himself. In fact, Rosen's statement did help him and it was because of it that Hoffman was released. Rosen had stated correctly that Hoffman had refused to let Peter, Fritz or Joseph stay with him, though he did not explain his motives, and by itself this would not sustain a conspiracy charge. The only witnesses against Hoffman were the landlady at 35 Newcastle Place and Tomacoff who had seen him, on separate occasions, in Fritz's lodgings;

but this proved nothing, as Hoffman did not deny acquaintanceship with Fritz. Obviously there was insufficient evidence against him and on 8 March the magistrates discharged him. The verdict had an exhilarating effect on the other prisoners. Vassilleva, Hoffman and Rosen were all smiles. At the back of the court Rosen's wife could be heard sobbing bitterly.

At the same time the magistrates released Sara Trassjonsky on similar grounds – that there was insufficient evidence against her. All the prisoners except her had been legally represented. She had presented a normal appearance to the court but her mind was continually clouding over. She explained through the interpreter that she wished to challenge some of the evidence, but could not remember what had been said the previous day; she also wanted to make some alterations and some additions to the statement the police had taken from her but had nobody to help her. The strain was too much, and when the charges were dropped and she suddenly found herself free after three months' imprisonment she became completely and hopelessly insane.

On 29 May 1911 the Solicitor for the London County Council wrote to the City Police Commissioner informing him that proceedings had been initiated at the instance of the L.C.C. with a view to deporting Sara Trassjonsky, who was being maintained as a pauper lunatic at Colney Hatch Asylum. She was summoned to appear at Bow Street magistrates' court, on 2 June, as being an alien in receipt of parochial relief and to show cause why an expulsion order should not be made against her under the Aliens Act, 1905. She was too ill to attend, but an order was granted for her deportation. The Clerk to the Asylums Committee told the police that she was insane, of suicidal tendencies and had to be tube fed, and that her condition was of such a nature that she might never recover sufficiently to be deported.

At the next hearing, on 15 March, Federoff's counsel challenged the prosecution's opening statement that the evidence would show that there had been a long-concerted and carefully planned conspiracy, and that each of the prisoners had been playing different but important parts in it. He had been carefully through the depositions and there was nothing to suggest that Federoff had taken part in this conspiracy. The witness Richardson alleged that he had seen Federoff on three occasions, firstly walking in Aldgate with Dubof and Peters, secondly standing with Peters at the corner of Aldgate, and thirdly on the morning of 13 December in the Three Nuns hotel. Even if what he said was true, which was denied, this was not proof of conspiracy. 'Conspiracies are not hatched in this manner, walking about the streets.' The other witnesses' evidence was equally doubtful. Bessie Jacobs, the teenaged girl from Exchange Buildings who had said nothing of Martin's cowardice, had picked out Federoff on an identification parade, but when she was asked to identify him in court had picked out Peters instead. She said that when she had picked him out the men had had their hats on; the male prisoners were given their hats and stood up again. She apologised for her mistake and correctly identified Federoff, but her credibility had gone. Her brother Harry, who had held the dying Sergeant Tucker, was also a prosecution witness, but when they left court with their expenses in their hands they saw their father standing on one corner of the Old Bailey and their mother on the other. Bessie was hit by her mother for giving her money to her father, and Harry was hit by his father for giving his money to his mother!

Federoff's council did not deny that his client had been at 59 Grove Street on the afternoon of 16 December. He was looking for work. Prosecuting counsel had said that it could be inferred what took place, but he submitted that you could not infer anything of the kind. Certainly Federoff knew Fritz but

if everybody who knew Fritz is presumed to have been implicated in this burglary, I am afraid his friends would not be safe. Hoffman knew Fritz and was seeing him constantly but this did not prevent you from discharging him. Federoff knew him. The other prisoner, Trassjonsky, has been discharged. She was acquainted with Fritz, and according to two or three witnesses was seen actually taking down the shutters and doing some work there. The fact that Trassjonsky had been seen in Exchange Buildings did not induce you to send her for trial. The evidence, such as it is, of

Federoff having been seen in Exchange Buildings, is not that upon which any jury would convict him.

The magistrate agreed and set him free. Federoff was the fourth prisoner to be discharged.

In a lull in the hearings prominent publicity was given to the christening of Sergeant Bentley's son Robert, named after his father, who had been born a few days after the shootings. The City Corporation made grants of five shillings a week to each of the murdered policemen's children until they were fifteen years of age. 'Baby' Bentley lived only three years and in 1914 was buried with his father. A *Daily Express* fund had raised nearly £2000 in four days for the policemen's dependants. Mrs Amelia Tucker and Mrs Louise Bentley, the widows of Sergeants Tucker and Bentley, were given pensions of thirty shillings a week so long as they remained widows and of good character. Miss Sylvia Choat, sister of Constable Choat, was given five shillings a week so long as she remained single. Sub-Inspector Bryant and Sergeant Woodhams, who had both been promoted, were presented with the Police Medal by the King. Woodhams had to be carried into the King's presence on a stretcher. His shattered leg had left him permanently crippled and Bryant, because of his chest wound, was also an invalid. Like Sergeant Leeson, who had been shot at the beginning of the 'siege', their promotions meant that they could be pensioned off at a higher rate. King's Police Medals were privately presented to the murdered policemen's families by the Lord Mayor.

At the same time as the committal proceedings, some of the witnesses and prisoners were also giving evidence at the Coroner's inquests on the bodies of the three policemen and Gardstein. Because the bodies had been taken to separate hospitals, they came under separate authorities, and the evidence had to be given in two courts – one in the City, which was holding an inquest on Sergeant Bentley, and one in the London Hospital, which was holding inquests on the other two policemen and Gardstein. Mr Bodkin drily remarked to one of the Coroners, 'The law is so strict, sir, that I believe if a body is found partly in one district and partly in another the inquest must be held in the district in which the head is.' Mr Bodkin, besides prosecuting at the magistrates' court, represented the Treasury at both inquests.

Inevitably the evidence fell into the same pattern and the wrong conclusions were drawn. Mr Wynne Baxter, the East London Coroner, in summing up, said, 'It had not been proved who actually shot Choat, but probably not Gardstein. With regard to the circumstances attending the death of Gardstein, no doubt the shot that caused his death was fired without any intention of hitting him, but that did not affect the crime. It was not accidental death, it was murder. All three of the persons, therefore, about whose death they were inquiring, were murdered.'

But he suggested that only in the case of Sergeant Tucker was there any evidence as to the personality of the murderer, and the jury brought a verdict of wilful murder against Gardstein. They found that Constable Choat and Gardstein had been wilfully murdered by some person or persons unknown. Subsequently the Coroner's jury at the City Court gave their verdict that Sergeant Bentley had been killed by Gardstein.

After these verdicts, the prosecution had to decide on the final charges against the four prisoners still in custody. Mr Bodkin asked that Peters and Dubof should be charged with murder. The principle was laid down in the Sissinghouse case

that where persons go out for an unlawful purpose in combination and if in the course of that combination it is determined to offer violent resistance to any who may hinder them in effecting that purpose and in the course of offering such resistance murder is committed by one of the combination, it is murder in all: and as to the two men, Peters and Dubof, there is evidence before you that within a few moments of this crime being committed they were there, found armed with similar weapons to those with which the murders were committed and in direct connection with one of the assailants, Gardstein.

The trial of the Houndsditch Murderers opened at the Old

Bailey on 1 May 1911 before Mr Justice Grantham. Nina Vassilleva looked pale as she stepped into the dock and moments later broke down and sobbed bitterly. Her tight-fitting black dress was shabby and a slouch hat of green tweed, with a feather, only emphasised her shabby appearance. She was charged with harbouring a felon guilty of murder, and with Peters and Dubof faced a further charge of conspiracy to break and enter. Peters had let his hair grow long and it was brushed back over his head. Rosen was charged with conspiracy to break and enter. They watched with interest as the jurors were sworn in and stared curiously at the sheriffs in their red gowns on the bench.

The court reporters could not remember a case in which there were so many exhibits. Sacks of exhibits, including the oxygen cylinder which had been bought for cutting the safe, were hauled into court by constables and detectives. On the solicitor's table was a perfectly scaled wood-model of Exchange Buildings and Harris's shop. On the plans the bullet holes and scars had been ringed in red.

Mr Bodkin's opening speech lasted two and a quarter hours. In a masterpiece of compression he went through the evidence, which the judge informed the court made 655 pages, and which had been collated and read – twice. After Max Weil and Constable Piper had given evidence he stopped Mr Bodkin from calling further witnesses and told him, to save time, that on the evidence this was not a case in which he could recommend the jury to find a verdict of guilty of murder. There was no evidence that either Peters or Dubof shot at the policemen, though it was assumed that they were there and it was possible that they did. 'You are within the law strictly, but we don't amplify charges of constructive murder in these days if we can help it.' In his view, it would be wiser to drop the charge of murder and go on with the charge of being accessory before the fact.

Mr Bodkin acceded to his suggestion and the judge directed the jury to say that the two men, against whom there was no evidence of shooting, were not guilty of murder. Peters and

Dubof nodded their heads as this was translated to them, but otherwise received the news with indifference.

The prosecution's chief witness was Isaac Levy (see above, p. 64). On 23 December he had picked Dubof and Peters, on an identification parade, out of a row of between fifteen and twenty others as the men who had been carrying Gardstein and had threatened him. He had afterwards picked out Vassilleva as the woman following him. Although, as the judge said, they could not reproduce a December night in May, two jurors went to Exchange Buildings, shortly before midnight the next day, to try a practical test. They wanted to see with certainty if a person could be identified as far as possible in the same conditions of light. In order that the experiment should be as faithful as possible the police took the precaution of seeing that all the lights in the narrow street were the same as on 16 December.

Two chance passers-by were stopped by the police and asked to walk past the two jurors who were stationed at the entrance to Exchange Buildings. Subsequently the two men were taken to Bishopsgate Police Station and put in a line-up to see if the jurors could pick them out. One juryman readily identified both men while the other identified one. One of the men who was wearing spectacles when he was seen by the jurors in Exchange Buildings, removed them before he was put in the line-up with the other men.

Levy came under a fierce attack from defence counsel. Mr Bodkin later complained of the venom and hostility he had been subjected to. But before this happened the judge intervened once more in an even more startling fashion. Mr Justice Grantham, on taking his seat, at the opening of the second day's hearing, said that since there was no other evidence of identification he could not allow any jury to find a verdict of guilty on Levy's uncorroborated statement! Therefore there was not sufficient evidence to justify the Crown pressing the case. Yet he thought there was other evidence to confirm Levy's statement that Vassilleva was the woman following Gardstein!

It is quite clear that she was a great friend of Gardstein.

In those circumstances there may well have been reason why she was following him. But yet she may have had no part in the shooting. Consequently, I think it would not be wise to press for a conviction against her as being an accessory after the fact of murder.

It does seem to me that assuming these were three people coming away from the scene, you are not in a position to say that they knew murder had been committed. The law is clear. You must show that an accessory after the fact knew that murder had been committed. Wounding is not murder. It may be a technical point; still it is a point to be taken into consideration. It is doubtful whether you could show that at that time they knew they were escaping from justice. It would not be safe, I think, for the Crown to press the case.

Mr Bodkin rose to his feet as another part of the Crown's case collapsed and said wearily,

While there was the evidence of the doctors that Sergeant Tucker must have died a minute or two after having been wounded, it was just possible that those who were there and saw Tucker might not have known that he was dead. There was another indictment preferred against the prisoners of being accessory after the fact of shooting Sergeant Bentley, but as the evidence of Levy would be the main point, his lordship's evidence as to that evidence would have an equal bearing on that charge.

He then withdrew the charge of being accessory after the fact; when this was translated to the prisoners and they were told that they had been found not guilty on that count either, the girl looked at the men and the men looked at her in some bewilderment. The only charge left against all four was conspiracy to break and enter.

Before the trial continued the judge dropped one more bombshell. He said he was strongly of the opinion, and he might be wrong, that three men, who were the chief murderers, had met their doom. Gardstein was clearly one of them. In his view the other two men were burnt in Sidney Street. 'There were three men firing shots and I think they are dead.' The prosecution

had to swallow this, but when the defence counsel for Federoff
and Peters stood up and said that it was only fair to the
prisoners to say that they had given the police all the assistance
and all the information in their power and that they had told
the police everything they were able to tell Mr Bodkin said
grimly, 'My friend had better not say that. It may provoke
an observation on my part.'

Out of the thirty or forty witnesses to be called, Isaac Levy's
evidence was the most damaging to the defence. The stout,
middle-aged man, firmly believing that his life was in jeopardy
by giving evidence, was subjected to a withering and sometimes
humiliating cross-examination, which left him reeling. He was
easily upset; his replies became more heated as counsel's cross-
examination steadily became more taunting and jeering; more
than once he had to be urged to be calm.

'This is the first time you have looked down the barrels of two
pistols, conceivably loaded,' counsel asked. 'Were you as composed then as you are now?' he asked. He turned as the judge,
intervening, said: 'Are you asking which is the worse – having
to face cross-examination or looking down the barrel of the
pistols?'

There was some laughter. Levy agreed that the experience
was 'a little out of the ordinary'.

'A little out of the ordinary! Did you run off like a hare?'

'I did not.'

'Did you say at the Guildhall that you ran away?'

'I was asked if I ran, and there was laughter among the
audience in court, and I said yes.'

'If people laugh you are willing to assent to a proposition?'

'I cannot pull a counsel up, and the question was not pushed
further or I should have explained that I was running towards
Exchange Buildings.'

In spite of the jeering cross-examination the defence could
not shake his evidence. Fortunately they did not have to now
that the judge had ruled that his uncorroborated evidence
was insufficient by itself to find a verdict of guilty. The defence
was further strengthened by a Crown witness, Constable

Martin, 'who stumbled and fell, and had such a miraculous escape'; he was asked by a juror if he had seen Levy near the scene of the occurrence. He answered quite truthfully he had not – though it was not for the reasons the juror supposed (see above, p. 57).

The defence submitted that there were only four conspirators, possibly five, and they were Gardstein, Fritz, Joseph, Max and possibly Peter the Painter. Further corroboration that this was so had been given in the magistrates' court by Luba Milstein and Karl Hoffman who, after their release, were called as witnesses for the defence. Luba swore that Fritz, Joseph and Max had brought Gardstein into the house, in spite of her earlier statement in which she said that she did not see the men come upstairs, and that two men left without her seeing them; she had made it, she said, because she did not want to give them away and was herself afraid of being charged. Hoffman's statement was even more astonishing. After his earlier statement denying that he knew most of the group or that anyone had come to his rooms after the murders, he completely reversed his evidence and said that Max had killed Gardstein, who was carried by Fritz and Max to Grove Street. Cross-examination was deferred, fortunately for him. He was not called any more, but if he had been he might have faced a criminal charge for such a blatant piece of perjury. He was fortunate, too, that his smuggled prison-notes to Dubof were not introduced into the evidence.

Dubof went into the witness box for nearly four hours. His real name, he explained, was Yourka Laiwin, but he had assumed the name of Dubof because he was a political refugee. He was twenty-four years old and the son of a small farmer. He had worked on the farm until he was eighteen and then went to Riga to learn painting. He returned to the farm in the autumn of 1905, when the revolt collapsed, but because he was an agitator he had to leave. He had been arrested and flogged with Cossacks' whips.

He explained that he had only gone to Grove Street on the afternoon of the sixteenth to see Peter the Painter about paint-

ing some decorations for the Lettish concert they were arrang-
ing. He had left at 4 p.m. and denied ever having been to
Exchange Buildings. Tomacoff unwillingly confirmed that while
he was there Dubof and Rosen were not conspiring to break
into a jeweller's shop. Dubof's principal witnesses were his
German landlady, the domineering Elsa Petter, who referred
to her lodger as 'my youngest baby', and twenty-six-year-old
Hans Bekov who worked, lived and slept with him and boasted
that since September there had only been two nights when they
had not slept together. In spite of this intimacy between all
three, neither Bekov nor Mrs Petter had any idea of the
existence of the group or who Dubof's friends were. In fact,
Mrs Petter, as she told the *Evening News* reporter before Dubof's
arrest, had made it a condition of his stay that he did not join
any anarchist clubs or belong to any political organisations.
Dubof, they said, had been home all evening and had gone to
bed with Bekov at 11.30 p.m. at the time of the murders, and
was still in bed when Bekov had got up at 6.45 the next
morning. They churned out dates, times and minutiae with
such mechanical efficiency, some of it going back four months,
that they were impregnable to cross-examination. For four
months they had tested each other and could not be shaken.

Rosen's defence was that he had paid friendly visits to Fritz,
glad to meet a fellow countryman and for the opportunity to
talk in his native tongue. He denied the construction that was
put on his visits. It was only two days after his wedding that
he was arrested and foolishly made the mistake of denying that
he knew Fritz. But two days later he repaired the damage by
telling all he knew. Similarly he denied ever being in Exchange
Buildings. It was a clear case of mistaken identity. His resemblance to Fritz was uncanny, particularly in profile, Hoffman
said. Fortunately for the defence this could be corroborated by
Tomacoff and Smolensky, Fritz's landlord in Newcastle Place,
who both thought that Fritz and Rosen were brothers.

Jacob Peters, giving evidence in his own defence, said that he
had been a grocer's assistant, a dock labourer and an employee
in a butter (oil) factory in Libau. For some years he was a

member of the Lettish Social Democratic Party and carried out propaganda work among the Army and the working classes.

'As a paid worker?' the judge asked.

'No, voluntarily. Only principal agitators get paid.'

He was arrested in Riga and held for eighteen months before being freed. Subsequently he went to Germany, intending to go to America, but he had insufficient money and found work in Germany. He next went to Denmark, but could not get work, and finally arrived in London in October 1909. He stayed with his cousin Fritz in Great Garden Street but eventually left him. He had expected him to be the same man (politically) as he was in Russia, but he had changed completely. Fritz professed to be an anarchist but knew nothing of anarchism. He had worked as a tailor's presser in Spitalfields from July 1910 until his arrest, but his alleged employers could never be found! Yet his defence counsel had handed the police a list, which he had from Peters himself, of the places where he was supposed to have worked.

In November 1910 Peters had joined an L.C.C. evening class for English but left because most of the pupils were Jews, and he had learnt more Yiddish than English. There was laughter when the judge said, 'I hope the London County Council will be aware of this. We can hardly call on the rate-payers to teach people Yiddish', which provoked another outburst. On 16 December he was at work all day and did not finish until after 8 p.m. He arrived at his lodgings about 9 p.m., and spent the rest of the evening repairing a mouse trap and reading. His landlord had last seen him a few minutes after 10 p.m., when he watched him set the mousetrap with a piece of cheese. Peters' room was on the ground floor facing the street – with two shutters, which were never bolted, over the window. As the landlord went out he saw the chinks of light at the top and bottom but when he returned at 11.30 p.m. the room was in darkness and he assumed Peters was in bed. This was the weak point in Peters' evidence. It was easy enough to infer that he had had ample time in which to get to Exchange Buildings, well before the murders, and later that night climb back into his room through the street window and the unbolted shutters.

But this damning suggestion was counter-balanced by the evidence that he rarely visited Grove Street and was not there on the afternoon of the sixteenth.

Nina's counsel faced a more formidable array of evidence. One witness after another told how she had dyed her hair, burned papers or tried to conceal them; of her distress at Gardstein's death, her blood-stained clothing, her attempts to get away to Paris. Richardson described seeing her in a miniature Merry Widow hat; the judge asked what he meant and he indicated the style of hat by holding his hands out two feet from his head. In the magistrates' court, she had aggressively challenged the evidence, particularly Levy's 'lies'. She was quieter now and frequently sobbed. Her counsel implied that she was a Jewish refugee from Russia where her father was a chef in the palace at St Petersburg. Since arriving in England four years before, when she was nineteen, she had earned a respectable living as a cigarette-maker. In his final summing-up, he said that the poor woman was in love with Gardstein, and she was under his influence, but there was nothing to prove that she knew anything of the conspiracy.

On the eleventh and final day, Mr Bodkin spoke up vigorously for the Crown's two principal witnesses, Levy and Richardson. The former had given his evidence in spite of the threats he feared on his life if he did so. As for Richardson, defence counsel had suggested that he was a dishonest employee because he had been sacked from his job; in fact, he had been sacked because of the time he had spent in court giving evidence. They had been singled out for 'venomous attack and hostile criticism'. How was crime to be repressed, Mr Bodkin asked, if witnesses who came forward were insulted.

In his summing-up which lasted an hour and a half, Mr Justice Grantham observed that if Constable Martin

had shown greater courage and a greater sense of duty on the occasion of the dreadful occurrences of 16 December he might have acted in a way that would have assisted the aims of justice. It was true that he was in great danger. The wounded man Gardstein must have been carried over the spot where Martin lay, and had Martin not been afraid to raise his head he must have seen who the persons were who were carrying Gardstein and been able to identify them without difficulty.

The police refused to believe that he was a coward or a liar.

One piece of evidence could not be explained away. In a cupboard, under the stairs, in 11 Exchange Buildings, the police had found two bottles with impressions from the right finger and thumb, including the scar on the forefinger, of Nina Vassilleva.

The jury found her guilty of conspiracy to break and enter but recommended that she should not be deported. The men were set free.

Nina was sentenced to two years' imprisonment, but five weeks later the Court of Appeal quashed her conviction on the ground of misdirection of the jury by Mr Justice Grantham!

Thus five months have passed since 16 December, when three constables of the City Police were murdered by a gang of armed alien burglars and two more policemen were seriously wounded. Not a single one of their assassins has been punished by the law. Gardstein, one of the murderers, was mortally wounded by a chance shot from one of his confederates. Two more of the gang perished in the Sidney Street 'battle' of January. But it is certain that the persons implicated were numerous. It is no pleasant or satisfactory reflection that several of the principals in the crime and many of their associates have escaped and are still at large.

The police can hardly be congratulated upon their success in dealing with this formidable conspiracy; but, in excuse, it must be remembered that in the vast alien population of East London it is a matter of peculiar difficulty to obtain evidence or run down the offender.*

* *Daily Mail*, 13 May 1911.

XI

Hero of October

ON 25 April 1911, before the trial ended, Max Smoller's wife left the house in Brick Lane, where she had moved from 1 Wellesley Street, and in St Katharine's Dock boarded a ship which was leaving the same night for Bremen. Police observers kept well in the background and watched two men walking about forty yards behind her. One of them the police knew and the other was a middle-aged man, of about fifty-five. Mrs Smoller was a distinctive figure in her long cream three-quarter-length coat and black hat, both of which flattered her plump, youthful figure and dark hair. Her children, Rachel, aged $5\frac{1}{2}$, with curly ginger hair to her shoulders, and Cecilia (Cissie), aged 3, were dressed in matching heliotrope dresses, white pinafores, bright red cloaks with hoods and black button boots. At the corner of Leman Street she shook hands with the two men and said goodbye. A young man of twenty-seven, the same age as herself, continued to push her luggage – a bundle wrapped in sacking – to the dock gates on a coster's barrow.

Her ticket had been bought in an assumed name. She told the Chief Officer that her husband had been in America for the past twelve months and that she herself was going to Russia. The ship sailed at 10 p.m. and with it the last traces of Max Smoller. He was never caught.

Nina Vassilleva felt very bitter towards him. In two wildly contradicting statements she made out that Gardstein's death hadn't been an accident. He had been deliberately murdered by Max, she said, who had organised the robbery for that very purpose! But there are so many obvious lies in both her statements that very little in either can be taken on trust. The only genuine thing was her grief for Gardstein.

Apart from Gardstein, the only feeling she showed for anyone was for Sara Trassjonsky, the hunchbacked little woman in Colney Hatch lunatic asylum. She sent her anonymously a small perfumed sachet pinned with a note 'To the nurse who so kindly tended Carl Gastin [Gardstein] in his last hours.' She ignored Luba Milstein; they had never been friends. In January 1912 Luba sailed for America and was not heard of again. Nina herself went back to cigarette-making and in the early sixties, when she was over seventy, was still living in a room by herself not far from the scene of the murders.

Of all those involved, Peter the Painter is the most firmly linked in the public's mind with the murders. Unquestionably he got his nickname from the fact that at times he earned his living as a painter and decorator. Unlike Yourka Dubof he did not have any artistic pretensions. A contemporary newspaper said, with what degree of truth we don't know, that 'Peter the Painter was colloquial Russian for "Bill Bailey" or "Will-o'-the-wisp", or any other name which indicates a disposition to disappear and reappear with tantalising frequency.' Certainly he lived up to his reputation and sightings were reported in America, Russia and Australia. But it would have been a pointless exercise to have followed up these leads, even if they had proved genuine, to have extradited him and brought him to trial. On the evidence the police had, he would never have been convicted. Mr Justice Grantham had made this quite plain at the trial when he stated that there was no evidence that Peter the Painter was one of the murderers.

From several sources it has been possible to flush out his elusive identity. The primary sources are two letters from the Sûreté in Marseilles and Paris, and some pencilled notes from an informant which further suggest that the Sidney Street informant was Charles Perelman.

On 23 May 1908 the Marseilles police raided No. 19 rue Chevalier Roze where there were a number of suspected refugees, among them Peter Piaktow, born at Pskow (Russia) on 20 June 1883 of Ivan and Marie Antonow. He described himself as a bachelor and a painter. On arriving in Marseilles he had gone to live at No. 11 rue d'Aubagne on 16 April 1908. At that time this house was reputed to be frequented by anarchists. From 7 June to 6 July 1908 he lived in No. 37 rue des Dominicaines (old No. 27). He then lived at No. 11 rue Ste Claire, and finally went to live in furnished rooms at No. 8 rue Chevalier Roze, the street where he had been arrested, from 4 October 1909 to 13 January 1910, at which time he left, saying he was going to Paris. Part of the time he worked as a painter at the rate of five francs a day.

According to the concierge of No. 37 rue des Dominicaines, Piaktow was a very violent character and often disappeared with his Russian friends, and finished by breaking with them. From a friend the police learned that he had abandoned his studies to work as a painter; that he had worked at the docks and at the Exhibition of Electricity, and had left at the end of 1909 for Évians-les-Bains. Somehow this friend was tricked into giving them other information: that Peter had been imprisoned for acts committed in the revolution of 1905 but had escaped and hidden in his birthplace with some friends, where he earned a living painting street doors, numbers, etc. His father had died in 1908 but his mother and sisters still lived at their farm somewhere near Talsen in Courland. He had travelled widely in Europe and said that he knew most of the countries.

He had studied chemistry in Switzerland but had to leave for an unexplained reason. While living in Marseilles, after his father's death, an uncle, who was an army colonel, told him that if he would go to Paris and study – not politics – he would send him money each month. He had come to Marseilles from Oran, shortly after the King of Portugal was assassinated, although there is no evidence that the two events were linked. He had arrived with a little Polish man, and lodged with him for a while, but the Pole was so lazy that they split up.

Somehow the Sûreté managed further to trick his friend into letting them borrow two photographs of Peter long enough for them to be copied, which the friend would certainly not have agreed to. They forwarded three copies of each pose to the City Police who, within two or three days of receiving them, issued a new 'wanted' poster reproducing both.

The Sûreté confirmed Peter's arrival in Paris from Marseilles, and added that he had lodged from 10 December 1909 to October 1910 at 4 rue Danville. From there he had gone to London.

Less than a week before they were given this news the City Police had been given another extraordinary piece of information. A Russian refugee called at the detective office and said that he believed that Peter the Painter was an anarchist, Peter Pilenas, who came from the same town as himself. He had come to England about four years previously and had first earned a living as a cap-maker and then by selling books on anarchism. He was then living in the neighbourhood of Commercial Street. This was about four years ago. Just after the murders, he had gone to live at a house in Bethnal Green but had stayed only a week, saying that he was going to live in Brooklyn, New York. His bombshell was that Peter Pilenas, whom he believed to be Peter the Painter, was the brother of Casimir Pilenas, who was the interpreter at the Thames Police Court, and whom the City Police had been using as an interpreter to interrogate and take statements from the Houndsditch murderers!

The official reaction is not known. Any damage Pilenas could have done would have been done already, if the story was true. Similarly we don't know if he made any official explanation confirming or denying the relationship, or whether the police simply ignored the information as too incredible to be believed. The first public hint of this story and its genuineness came in 1934 with the publication of Sergeant Leeson's memoirs and was finally confirmed in 1967 by Nina Vassilleva's firm of solicitors.

Leeson's source was a letter from Casimir Pilenas written to him some years after the 'siege', certainly after 1916. Unfortunately he does not explain why it should have been written to him. He merely quotes three brief extracts, and the rest of the letter is built into his story. Casimir Pilenas is not identified by name, but Leeson says that 'this man', though brother to the 'Painter', actually worked for the forces of law and order against Peter and his gang. Casimir Pilenas denied that his brother had been involved in the murders and Leeson further quotes: 'My brother Peter, whose name appeared in some of the documents of the Houndsditch murder case, was here already. So I joined him. He did not live very long; he died in the summer of 1914 [sic]* in Philadelphia. . . .'

In the late thirties Sir William Crocker – his father had represented Sara Trassjonksy and Nina Vassilleva – was on business in New York, where he met again Casimir Pilenas. Casimir told him the 'truth' about Peter the Painter, who he said was his brother, Peter Pilenas. In his memoirs Sir William published a photograph of Peter Pilenas taken between 1911 and 1916 when he died in Philadelphia; the date of his death is given as 17 August, although the body was too badly decomposed to determine how and when he died. The photograph is marked 'Peter the Painter'.

According to Sir William Crocker the Houndsditch murderers tried to blame the innocent Peter the Painter for the murders by putting the dying Gardstein in his room instead of in Fritz's to draw the suspicion away from the real killers. This doesn't make sense as both rooms were rented and lived in by Fritz – Peter was only staying with him. In fact, Peter Pilenas had already left for America and was at sea on the day of the murders.

Was his story genuine? Was Peter the Painter in fact Peter Pilenas? If not, why should Casimir Pilenas say he was?

The evidence is against them being the same man. Peter Pilenas was making caps and selling anarchist literature in England when Peter Piaktow was in prison after the 1905 revolution and in hiding at Pskow in Russia; besides Pilenas was seven years older than Piaktow, and their photographs show that they were not the same man. Certainly there is a

---

* It was in fact 1916; see below.

strong likeness between them; but there was also a likeness between Fritz Svaars and John Rosen (see above, page 163).

To begin with, the hairline is different. Pilenas has more hair, though this could be explained by a wig. What cannot be concealed is the nose and ears. Even allowing for the slightly different pose, it is clear that Peter Piaktow has a much thicker bridge to his nose and that the ears are a different shape.

But why should Casimir Pilenas say that his brother was Peter the Painter? When the police were told of his relationship with Peter Pilenas, he must have been questioned closely and have been able to satisfy them that his brother was not the Painter. It is inconceivable that he would have been allowed to continue as one of the interpreters if he had not been able to do so, and it is equally inconceivable that the police ignored the information. Yet after his brother's death, and when he himself had emigrated to America, he wrote to the credulous Sergeant Leeson, whom he knew from their East End days, claiming that his brother and Peter Piaktow were the same man. He volunteered this information not only to Leeson but to Sir William Crocker as well, neither of whom had previously suspected the relationship, and both published it in good faith, Leeson (at Pilenas' request) without giving his source. If Pilenas was anxious for the story to be believed, why did not he publish it himself? The answer must be that he daren't because it was not true. The police would immediately have denied it; one can just hear the jeers if they hadn't: while they were hunting Peter the Painter his brother was interpreting for them and helping the killers to go free. No, Peter Pilenas was not Peter the Painter, but Casimir Pilenas would have liked people to believe the legend that he was.

He also made another claim which, at first, sounds far more incredible. Leeson quotes it in his memoirs: '. . . but the crime itself was organised by Stalin, now head of the Soviet Government.'

Why? The clue is Jacob Peters, the man who should have hanged for murdering three City of London policemen.

When Pilenas wrote his letters the former tailor's-presser was one of the most powerful men in Stalinist Russia and a former Deputy Chairman of the terrible Cheka – the All Russian Extraordinary Commission for Combating Counter-Revolution and Sabotage. A recent Soviet biography* comments: 'Yakov Peters. That name aroused fear and hatred in foes of the Revolution, in spies and saboteurs. They said of him: he is Dzerzhinsky's right hand.'

In exile, from 1909 to 1917, Peters had been an active member of the Latvian Social Democratic Party London group. He opposed the Menshevik Central Committee, and in the summer of 1912 succeeded in establishing an L.S.D. Bolshevik Foreign Bureau in London. The revolution of February 1917 opened up the road to Russia for Peters, and the Foreign Bureau sent him back as its representative. In Petrograd he was made a member of the Bolshevik Military Organisation and was sent to Latvia to agitate and propagandise among the Lettish battalions, as he had done in 1905. He seized every opportunity to spread propaganda among the soldiers, and spoke at meetings, conferences, demonstrations and funerals. He became one of the editors of a Bolshevik Latvian newspaper and did not hesitate to unmask, ridicule and morally destroy his enemies.

When support for the Bolsheviks waned and Lenin went into hiding Peters continued to agitate for Bolshevik support. On 23 September 1917 he opened and presented the main report to the 14th Conference of the Latvian Territory Social Democratic Party held in Valka. He spoke of the coming revolution, of the inevitable victory of the working class. He urged that only convinced Bolsheviks should be sent to the Second All Russian Congress of Soviets. 'The situation is grave and time is ripe. We must take power in our hands, save Russia and call the peoples to fight a revolutionary battle all over Europe.' The Latvian delegates sent him as their delegate to the congress where he was elected a member of the All Russian Central Executive Committee.

* *Geroi Oktiabria* (*Heroes of October*) (Leningrad, 1967) vol. 2, pp. 234–5.

He was included in the Military Revolutionary Committee of the Petrograd Soviet, which in fact masterminded the October *coup d'état* and Bolshevik seizure of power. Two months after the October revolution the Cheka was formed to combat counter-revolution; Peters was appointed Deputy Chairman to the fanatical Dzerzhinsky.

In March 1918, the Cheka was moved to Moscow following the transfer there of the Soviet Government from Petrograd. The Muscovites were lukewarm in their support; the Mensheviks, anarchists and other political groups were openly agitating against Bolshevik authority, gathering support from the tens of thousands of soldiers arriving from the front. Since the Bolsheviks were unable to feed them they started to loot. The main opposition came from the anarchist Black Guard who, Peters recalled, 'issued orders as if they were in authority, rounded people up on the streets, took away weapons and valuables, and handed out the bourgeois rags right and left to the people'. On one occasion the Black Guard seized a large quantity of opium, sold it and used the money to publish the anarchist newspaper *Chernoye Znamya* ('Black Banner'). Later, the Bolsheviks discovered that the Black Guard were also being issued with rifles, bombs and machine-guns from the Moscow Military Commissariat. Within a month, the Cheka was ready to liquidate it.

On 13 April, at 3 a.m., simultaneous attacks were made on the Black Guard headquarters and twenty-five other centres, and their influence was totally destroyed. More than 100 people were killed, and 500 arrested. Later in the day, Peters escorted the British diplomat Robert Bruce Lockhart through the fighting areas. In house after house they entered, the filth was indescribable. Formerly these houses had belonged to wealthy people, but now broken bottles littered the Aubusson carpets; paintings had been slashed, priceless heirlooms and ornaments lay smashed on the ground. Ceilings were punctured with bullet holes and the bodies were still lying where they had fallen.

In the luxurious drawing-room of the House Gracheva the

Anarchists had been surprised in the middle of an orgy. The long table which had supported the feast had been over-turned, and broken plates, glasses, champagne bottles, made unsavoury islands in a pool of blood and spilt wine. On the floor lay a young woman, face downwards. Peters turned her over. Her hair was dishevelled. She had been shot through the neck, and blood had congealed in a sinister purple clump. She could not have been more than twenty. Peters shrugged his shoulders. 'Prostitutka,' he said. 'Perhaps it is for the best'.*

Although it had no justification in law, this action further confirmed the Cheka's right to carry out summary executions. In February 1918 it announced that it saw 'no other way to combat counter-revolutionaries, spies, speculators, burglars, hooligans, saboteurs and other parasites than their merciless annihilation at the scene of the crime'. Later in the year it un-leashed 'mass red terror'. The following year Peters was described as a mere furious animal, signing death warrants all day, often without looking to see what he was signing; he earned the sobriquet 'Executioner' because of the number it was said he carried out with his own hands.

When, in July and August 1918, the Left Socialist Revo-lutionaries revolted, assassinating the German Ambassador and seizing Dzerzhinsky and Latsis, Peters played a major part in putting them down and restoring Bolshevik control. Numerous executions followed the Bolshevik recapture of towns and cities momentarily seized in the July rebellion. As the civil war heightened so the terror increased. The Tsar and his family were murdered at Ekaterinburg. The next month it was the turn of the Bolshevik leaders. On the morning of 30 August, the head of the Petrograd Cheka was murdered, and the same evening a young woman tried to assassinate Lenin as he left a Moscow factory and wounded him with two bullets. Arrests began in Petrograd on a massive scale. Robert Bruce Lockhart, who had been shown by Peters the anarchist headquarters on the day the

* Bruce Lockhart, *Memoirs of a British Agent*.

Black Guard was liquidated, was among those arrested. He had been approached by Cheka *agents provocateurs* with offers to bribe the Lettish regiments to turn against the Bolsheviks. Bruce Lockhart had put them in touch with the British Secret Service and was now heavily implicated in the plot. He was bundled out of bed and taken to Lubianka No. 11, which was the head-quarters of the Moscow Cheka. After a long wait he was taken along a dark corridor and shown into a long dark room lit only by a hand-lamp on the writing-table.

At the table, with a revolver lying beside the writing-pad, was a man, dressed in black trousers and a white Russian shirt. His black hair, long and waving as a poet's, was brushed back over a high forehead. There was a large wrist-watch on his left hand. In the dim light his features looked more sallow than ever. His lips were tightly compressed, and, as I entered the room, his eyes fixed me with a steely stare. He looked grim and formidable. It was Peters.

Lockhart was released almost immediately, but a few days later was re-arrested and imprisoned for exactly one month in the Lubianka where he had frequent conversations with Peters. Peters apologised for the food – soup, tea and potatoes – but it was the same as that supplied to himself.

When he had a free moment, he liked discussing England, the war, capitalism and revolution. He told me strange tales of his experiences as a revolutionary. He had been in prison in Riga in Tsarist days. He showed me his nails as a proof of the torture which he had undergone. There was nothing in his character to indicate the inhuman monster he is commonly supposed to be. He told me that he suffered physical pain every time he signed a death sentence. I believe it was true. There was a strong streak of sentimentality in his nature, but he was a fanatic as far as the clash between Bolshevism and Capitalism was concerned, and he pursued his Bolshevik aims with a sense of duty which was relentless.

As we were talking, a motor van – a kind of 'Black Maria' – pulled up in the court-yard below, and a squad of men, armed with rifles and bandoliers, got out and took up their places in the yard. Presently a door opened just below us, and three men with bowed heads walked slowly forward to the van. I recognised them instantly. They were Sheglovitoff, Khvostoff, and Bieletsky, three ex-Ministers of the Tsarist regime, who had been in prison since the revolution. There was a pause followed by a scream. Then through the door the fat figure of a priest was half-pushed, half-carried, to the 'Black Maria'. His terror was pitiful. Tears rolled down his face. His knees rocked, and he fell like a great ball of fat on the ground. I felt sick and turned away. 'Where are they going?' I asked. 'They are going to another world,' said Peters drily. 'And that man', he said pointing to the priest, 'richly deserves it.' It was the notorious Bishop Vostorgoff. The ex-Ministers formed the first batch of the several hundred victims of the Terror who were shot at that time as reprisal for the attempted assassination of Lenin.*

Peters wrote later that about 600 people were shot by the Moscow Cheka alone.

In less than one year the Cheka, not exceeding 500 men, had crushed two large plots and the uprising of the Leftish Social Revolutionaries. By the autumn of 1918 public attention had turned to the mounting attacks of the White Guard on the different fronts, and there was a relative calm internally. Opponents of the Cheka tried to prove it was no longer necessary and pressed for its replacements by courts. The Cheka had to withstand many such attacks in the Press, and also at party meetings and conferences. But it survived and Peters later wrote that it became 'necessary to mete out justice at a much more ferocious rate than in 1918'. Earlier he implied that they did not shoot enough people in the first year because they were too inexperienced. The official figure, which is thought to be an underestimate, for the first year's work is 6300.

Before Bruce Lockhart left Russia in October 1918, Peters asked him if he would give a letter and photographs to the woman he had married in 1912 in England. She was a young good-looking woman and they had a daughter Mary. Several

* R. H. Bruce Lockhart, *op. cit.*

times Mrs Peters was offered a chance to rejoin her husband but she was reluctant to leave her home for the uncertainty of Russia. When eventually she did go to Moscow she found that Peters had divorced her and married again.

Lenin thought Peters a 'brilliant and very dependable man'. From 1919 to 1922 he held a number of appointments including that of Commander of the internal defence of Petrograd when General Yudenitch's regiments were advancing on the city, and in August 1919 Commander of the Kiev fortified area with Voroshilov and Latsis as members of its council. In October Zinoviev and Trotsky sent a telegram to Lenin in Moscow urging that Peters should be immediately sent to Petrograd, which was being menaced by White troops.

Peters was the Cheka Plenipotentiary in Turkestan. In 1930 he carried out purges of the Red Army.

In December 1937 English newspapers reported that Peters had been arrested in the Stalin purges, together with the Chief of the Soviet Air Force and others. Soviet sources differ as regards the date of his death when he was executed. In 1948 his English daughter Mary, who was working for the British Embassy in Moscow, was kidnapped. She disappeared until the early sixties when she was apparently released.

In recent years, the date is uncertain, Peters has been re-habilitated; the revolutionary ex-tailor's presser, who should have hanged in 1911 for murdering three English policemen, is now a Hero of October. 'His educators were the party and revolution, and he served them loyally and was a model soldier for the socialist homeland.'

Postscript: Some Other Misconceptions

APART from the mystery of Peter the Painter, there are two stories which are consistently linked with the murders and the 'siege'. They are the murder of Leon Beron and a persistent rumour which nothing, it seems, will dispel that Stalin masterminded the Houndsditch murders.

Briefly, Leon Beron's body was found on Clapham Common on New Year's Day. On his face were some cuts vaguely suggesting an 'S'. At the trial of Steinie Morrison, who was convicted of the murder, his defence counsel tried to suggest that the 'S' stood for 'Spy' and that Leon Beron had been killed for betraying Fritz and Joseph. The major theorist for this argument is J. B. Holroyd in *The Gaslight Murders*.

The only evidence I have discovered for Holroyd's theory is the following document which was written to the Deputy Medical Officer at Brixton Prison on 28 January 1911 by Warder T. Russel: 'As Prisoner – S. Morrison – was leaving the Hospital for discharge this morning, Prisoner Y. Dubof came towards him and remarked, "Wish you success".'

Since they were both awaiting trial this can hardly be construed as anything sinister or implicating them in each other's crime. As for the cuts on Beron's face: if, in fact, it was an 'S' on either cheek, it is much more likely that it stood for 'Jew' as this was how the letter was interpreted in one of the smuggled prison-notes (see above, page 139).

Leon Beron did not betray Fritz and Joseph. But could he have been killed because he was an informer? The answer must be firmly in the negative. And it is possible to be so certain because of how the group – those who were free – reacted to

Nicholas Tomacoff. If anyone should have been killed for
betraying Fritz and Joseph it was Tomacoff. He had gone
voluntarily to the police; his information had already led to two
arrests; several days before Beron's murder, he was being pointed
out as a police informer to a salesman, who warned the police
on 28 December. What is equally clear from the salesman's
statement is that Tomacoff was still playing in the concerts and
clubs where he did not have the protection of the policeman.
One can safely say, on this evidence, that Beron was not killed
because he was an informer and that whatever the motive for
killing him – the prosecution maintained it was robbery – there
is nothing to link his death with either the Houndsditch murders
or the 'siege'.

The most recent source for the Stalin theory has been Richard
Deacon's *A History of the Russian Secret Service*. Any credibility in the theory is completely destroyed by his opening
account of the 'siege'.

> This incident which resulted in a five-hour rifle battle between
> Anarchists and Scots Guards provided an excellent example
> of Russian counter-espionage techniques as used abroad. A
> police sergeant, investigating a report of 'strange noises'
> coming from a house in Sidney Street, Houndsditch, called
> there and was shot dead. When other police surrounded the
> house and demanded that the occupants surrendered they
> were met by a barrage of fire from automatic pistols. Two
> more police were shot dead and Winston Churchill, then
> Home Secretary, ordered out the Scots Guards to assist the
> police. One thousand police, supported by Guards, kept up a
> fire on the house, which was eventually burnt down.

He goes on to quote a Mr James Burley who claimed that he
regularly went to the Continental Café, in Little Newport
Street, Soho, which Stalin also used a lot in 1910. 'Jozef Georgi
he called himself. He was a bombastic little man, not very big.'
Mr Burley claimed that Stalin knew all about the events leading
up to the 'siege', that he was looked up to as one of the leaders,

that he had a hand in planning the burglary and that he kept a watch on Peter the Painter.

In fact, the earliest anyone could have started planning the robbery was in May 1910 when the shop opened. Stalin's movements can be traced for this period and have been confirmed by Soviet as well as Western historians. He was arrested on 23 March 1910 and transferred to a prison in Baku three days later. Six months later, on 23 September, he was taken under escort to Solvychegodsk in northern Russia – which was later one of Stalin's central N.K.V.D. concentration camps. He was still there in July 1911. Nor is it likely that he would or could have masterminded the robbery by letter at this distance, or that he would have hesitated to betray an anarchist plot to the Ochrana, when he was already betraying the Bolsheviks to them with whom he was linked politically and trying to gain favour. The theory that he was involved in the 'siege' just won't stand up. Obviously its genesis was Pilenas' letter, quoted by Leeson, which was written when Stalin was head of the Soviet State and Peters one of its most powerful men. It has been believed because of Stalin's short stay in London in 1907 and his involvement in the expropriation at Tiflis soon after.

There is one final theory that the Houndsditch robbery was masterminded by an *agent provocateur* of the Tsarists to provoke them into expropriations which would bring them to the notice of the police and ensure their deportation to Russia. Peter the Painter is generally credited with being the *agent provocateur* and is allowed to escape with the connivance of the police and the intelligence service. Again this overlooks the basic fact that political refugees were not deported – not even, judging by Nina Vassilleva, after a criminal conviction in this country and when they were wanted on a capital charge in their own. Perhaps now some of the mystery will be allowed to die down.

Select Bibliography

Churchill, Randolph S., *Winston S. Churchill*, vol. 2, *Young Statesman 1901–1914* (Heinemann, 1967).

Churchill, Winston S., *Thoughts and Adventures* (Odhams Press, 1932).

Crocker, William Charles, *Far from Humdrum* (Hutchinson, 1967).

Deacon, Richard, *A History of the Russian Secret Service* (Frederick Muller, 1972).

Eddy, J. P., *The Mystery of 'Peter the Painter'* (Stevens, 1946).

Harcave, Sidney, *First Blood* (Macmillan, 1964).

Hassall, Christopher, *Edward Marsh* (Longmans, 1959).

Hastings, Macdonald, *The Other Mr Churchill* (Harrap, 1963).

Hingley, Ronald, *The Russian Secret Police* (Hutchinson, 1970).

Holroyd, James Edward, *The Gaslight Murders* (Allen & Unwin, 1960).

Leeson, Benjamin, *Lost London* (Stanley Paul, 1934).

Linklater, Eric, *The Corpse on Clapham Common* (Macmillan, 1971).

Lockhart, R. H. Bruce, *Memoirs of a British Agent* (Putnam, 1932).

—, *My Europe* (Putnam, 1952).

London, Jack, *The People of the Abyss* (Nelson, 1903).

Macnaghten, Sir Melville, *Days of My Years* (Edward Arnold, 1915).

Moorehead, Alan, *The Russian Revolution* (Collins/Hamish Hamilton, 1958).

Nicholls, Ernest, *Crime within the Square Mile* (John Long, 1935).

Nott-Bower, Sir William, *Fifty Two Years a Policeman* (Edward Arnold, 1926).

Pope, A. U., *Maxim Litvinoff* (Secker & Warburg, 1943).

Rose, Millicent, *The East End of London* (Cresset Press, 1951).

Serge, Victor, *Memoirs of a Revolutionary 1901–1941* (Oxford University Press, 1963).

Seth, Ronald, *The Russian Terrorists* (Barrie & Rockliff, 1966).

—, *The Executioners* (Cassell, 1967).

Shub, David, *Lenin* (Pelican, 1966).

Sinclair, Robert, *East London* (Robert Hale, 1950).

Smith, Edward Ellis, *The Young Stalin* (Cassell, 1931).

Ulam, Adam B., *Lenin and the Bolsheviks* (Secker & Warburg, 1966).

Wensley, F. P., *Detective Days* (Cassell, 1931).

Wolin, Simon, and Slusser, Robert M., *The Soviet Secret Police* (Praeger, 1957).

Wood, Walter, *Survivors' Tales of Famous Crimes* (Cassell, 1916).

Woodcock, George, *Anarchism* (Pelican, 1963).

Index